MINISTRY TO THE DIVORCED

MINISTRY TO THE DIVORCED

GUIDANCE, STRUCTURE, AND
ORGANIZATION THAT PROMOTE
HEALING IN THE CHURCH

Sue Poorman Richards
and
Stanley Hagemeyer

Zondervan Publishing House • Grand Rapids, MI

MINISTRY TO THE DIVORCED

Copyright © 1986 by
Sue Poorman Richards and Stanley Hagemeyer

MINISTRY RESOURCES LIBRARY
is an imprint of
Zondervan Publishing House
1415 Lake Drive S.E.
Grand Rapids, Michigan 49506

Library of Congress Cataloging in Publication Data

Richards, Sue Poorman
    Ministry to the divorced.

        Bibliography: p.
        1. Church work with divorced people. I. Hagemeyer, Stanley. II. Title.
BT707.H34   1986   261.8'3589   86-8389
ISBN 0-310-20051-2

Masculine pronouns are sometimes used generically in instances where gender is indeterminate.

Edited by James E. Ruark

Printed in the United States of America

86 87 88 89 90 91 92 93 94 / 11 10 9 8 7 6 5 4 3 2 1

CONTENTS

PART I

PART II

PART I

1

THE TRAGIC REALITY

Nobody expects on that sweet day when vows are exchanged that one day the vows will be shattered and two people will become a divorce statistic. I certainly didn't. And I have the feeling that, of the 378,000 other American couples involved in divorces in the first quarter of 1983, none supposed they would become divorce statistics either. According to the 1984 World Almanac *"Vital Statistics," the marriage rate per 1,000 population during the same period in 1983 was 4.9. The rate of divorce was climbing to more than half the number of marriages. A staggering 1,178,000 divorces were recorded in 1983, down slightly from the 1982 figure of 1,180,000. Calculated: the number of divorced people in the United States grew in 1982–83 by a stunning 4,716,000.*

Unfortunately divorce affects more people than just those who exchanged vows. The same "Vital Statistics" show that the number of one-parent families doubled from 3.3 million in 1970 to 6.6 million in 1981 when they comprised 20 percent of the nation's 31.6 million families with children present. Nearly three-fourths of all people maintaining such families were separated or divorced. This adds up to additional millions of hurting, bleeding, and angry people who need to feel the love of God lift and support them, often through the hands of their brothers and sisters in Christ.

Divorce is the death of a relationship. It is the severing of ties that make two people one. It usually leaves a person somehow disfigured emotionally yet strangely unchanged physically. —Sue

JILL AND JOHN

Jill and John are a typical example of a couple who have experienced a divorce. They were a Christian family. John was an upper-level executive in a major U.S. corporation. Jill worked odd jobs while

9

caring for their young family so John could continue his studies at the University of Michigan. They had more than ten years in counseling, but it failed to produce reconciliation and forgiveness.

After twenty-six years of struggling, raising four children and supporting them through college, Jill and John divorced. The marriage ended, accompanied by much pain. Only the remnants of hurt, anger, and disbelief remain. John surely suffered, yet for him the transition went quite well, or so it would seem. He retained the family home, furniture, camping equipment—he could afford to. He still had his lucrative career. Soon after the divorce he met a nice Christian woman and remarried.

For Jill the transition wasn't so easy. She had just finished her B.A. a couple of years before the divorce. Although she had worked to offset college expenses for the children while attending her own classes and trying to manage the home, her earning capacity is small. The money in settlement helped, but it hasn't been enough, and it's been hard to get John to pay support, now that he has new obligations. Jill finds herself working two or three part-time jobs, trying desperately to be a financially self-sufficient person. She talks to her minister, reads Christian books, teaches Sunday school, and prays for strength to survive each day.

We pray for Jill. That God will hold her up. That she will feel his arms around her and not give in to those drifting thoughts of suicide. She lives several hundred miles away, so we have faith that others will help her bear her burdens as Christ would have us do.

Jill has had several car accidents since her divorce. The last one was quite serious even though it involved only her car. It was near the holidays; she was depressed and lonely. Christmas would never again be Mom and Dad with their children and three little grandchildren around the fireplace. John and his new wife would be enjoying her children and grandchildren near the fireplace instead. Ironically, many feel a heightened sense of alienation and loss through the holidays—days when their focus turns inward, bringing pain and depression.

After the accident Jill realized it wasn't so accidental. She had been driving along thinking how difficult the struggle to survive had become. She wondered if it was really worth it. She began to cry, and as she lost control of herself she also lost control of her car on the snowy pavement. Jill is getting therapy now and seems to be making some positive choices about life. But her struggle isn't over.

No divorce is just like any other. Because God made each of us unique, we all have different situations, different personalities, and different ways of dealing with stressful situations. Here are some people in our community. They have problems similar to the people in yours.

DOLORES

Dolores, a middle-aged woman with one daughter, has her own set of problems. She doesn't know what to do with herself. Dolores and her husband had been married for twenty-eight years when he packed his bags, announcing he didn't want to be married to her any longer. Dolores feels lost. She told us, "When he wanted his laundry done, he told me and I'd do it. When he woke up and said he wanted molasses cookies, I'd bake molasses cookies. I don't know what to do anymore."

As time passed, we gave emotional support to Dolores and often assured her that she was growing. She surprised us with her tearful reply, "I don't want to grow, I don't want to make it. He said I could make it and he always told me he was right." To comfort her, someone replied that it must have been easier for her with her husband there to guide her decisions. At that, Dolores, a shy, soft-spoken woman, piped up with a spark and said, "Oh no. It hasn't been easy to always be wrong."

Dolores *is* growing. We have hope that with others supporting her and praying for her, Dolores will someday be willing to be the person God gave her the potential to be. She's not a simple-minded thing who needs to be told what to do. God gave her a mind and a compassionate heart. But her struggle to grow will be full of pain, and there may still be years of setbacks and loneliness ahead.

GREG

Greg was a deacon in his church. He thought that divorce was something that happened to non-Christians. He was a school principal who owned two boats, two cars, a home, and a summer home. He was a pillar in the church and the community. Then Greg experienced the agony of divorce. His church not only took his position from him, but asked him to worship elsewhere. To his fellow church members, Greg's divorce was an unforgivable sin.

Greg felt lost. Unforgiven. Indeed, he was unforgiven—not by the Lord, but by himself and others who had taken it upon themselves to judge a brother. The burden of his guilt nearly overwhelmed him.

LIL

Lil had been married eight and a half years when her husband announced he could no longer grow and be himself while bound in their marriage. Lil was four months pregnant with their third child. Their first had died during a complicated breech delivery. Their second child, a strong-willed son, was three. Lil had to begin working when her baby was a year old. She hated leaving her children with a baby-sitter.

Two years later Lil remarried. Her second marriage is wonderful, for her and for the children. But the pain and ugly reality of Lil's divorce still pierces her heart and the hearts of her children each time Daddy comes from out of state for a visit. The children are always excited to see him, and they grieve when he leaves. Once after the family took him to the airport, seven-year-old Joshua wept bitterly, saying, "When Daddy isn't here, I forget how much I miss him."

Lil and her children feel that pain over and over again. Lil looks on helplessly as her children grieve again and again for the man she once grieved for. She is overwhelmed with guilt because she knows they are innocent of any wrongdoing that led to the breakdown in her marriage. Her children will pay all their lives for her mistakes and their father's. And each time her children pay, a little piece of her heart is torn and she pays once again. Even under the best of circumstances, when children are involved, the heartbreak of divorce never ends. The intensity will fade through the years as the wounds heal, but things will never be the same.

REALITY PLUS HOPE

Divorce is a painful process. Many who go through divorce do not want it, but are forced into facing its ugly reality, the numbness it brings, and the loneliness, the terrible loneliness. In a sense, there is often no final resolution to the pain divorce brings. People must learn to live with it as a thorn in the flesh.

We can trust that God's grace really is sufficient and that it can bring effective resolution and renewal. We have to be sensitive to the reality of the pain people bear, and then hope with them that God is able to use even this.

Each day that passes sees more marriages ending. It is a fact that would be convenient to push into a closet if we were free to ignore it. But we are not. We are called to bear one another's burdens and to love one another as Christ loves us. That means that we have a responsibility toward those who are suffering in divorce. And learning ways to fulfill that task is the subject of this book.

2
NEEDS THE CHURCH CAN MEET

How is the Christian community responding to those mourning the death of their marriage? There are probably as many answers to this question as there are Christians in the world. We feel it would be helpful, however, to characterize the church's responses in three ways: hurting, ignoring, and healing.

Probably the most hurtful way the Christian community can minister is in being judgmental. The attitude that "real" Christians don't get divorced is a terrible stumbling block to ministering to real Christians who get divorced.

Being judgmental will not edify the ministry of forgiveness that Jesus modeled for us. Jesus associated with the undesirables of his time. The unique quality of his healing ministry was that the King came to serve and heal the needy, the sick, and the lost.

Another negative approach of ministry is to ignore. "We don't have that many singles, so we really can't justify a program for them." "Our main thrust is families. That's where most of our congregation is. The rest will just have to fit in where they can."

But the church can't stop there. The problem of what to do with singles isn't vanishing. Rather, it is increasing.

It's okay not to have a singles program, but the church must then find out where to refer singles for various activities: social, Bible study, sharing, therapy. We will suggest how to be sensitive in making singles feel welcome instead of just "fitting" in. And in chapter 5 we will help you decide if your church needs a special program and, if so, what type of singles activities would fit its needs.

A positive ministry can make a tremendous difference to suffering people. Here are some examples of how a positive ministry can help those going through a divorce.

DUANE AND BARB

Duane and Barb were members of a small church. Duane wasn't sure how the church would respond when Barb left him. One board member who didn't know them very well made a point of meeting with each of them for coffee or other occasions he could arrange that would provide some time to get to know them. He spent the first few contacts inquiring respectfully and listening intently. He indicated that he cared about both parties and respected their struggle with important life issues. He made his family home available to each of them, encouraging them to drop in any time, even extending an open dinner invitation requiring just short notice.

At other times, the board member and his wife would baby-sit when Barb needed a break or assist her in shopping for a new refrigerator when the old one quit. Eventually he gained their confidence and could confront both Duane and Barb with painful and searching questions. Each struggled and grew personally. They were not reunited, but they were helped through their most troubled and stressful year of separation.

This man's instinctive Christian love and support reflected the quality of a professional counselor's training, but remarkably he wasn't even a high school graduate. Both Duane and Barb eventually moved on to different churches, but this layman's wisdom and patience had filled the gap of Christian fellowship in a way that helped both of them to maintain a sense of dignity and confidence in the people of God.

ARLENE

Arlene's situation was quite different from Barb and Duane's. She was an active member of a large church with a city-wide membership. Her husband was not a Christian, although he did attend worship occasionally to please her during their earlier married years. He eventually grew more openly critical of her faith and adamant in expressing his own agnostic views. He was an intelligent professional, and his career goals dominated his life.

Arlene's need to seek meaning in her church and children grew. She sensed that her marriage was sliding downhill rapidly. After almost twenty years of marriage, he moved out. She did not know who to turn to within the church she loved.

The pastor directed Arlene to a small counseling center that had been established a few years earlier as an adjunct ministry of the church. She learned that small groups of separated and divorced persons met regularly there for support and group therapy. The costs were much less than individual counseling required. People from many different churches took part. Each group was limited to about eight or ten participants. There was an agenda that the counselor used to guide the group along to specific goals appropriate to divorce recovery, but the group was never hurried. Mutual support was a key element in the healing process.

A few months later, Arlene thanked her pastor for his suggestion. This quiet, low-profile element within the large church's total ministry was the lifeline that was needed for her recovery. Her love and loyalty to God and His church were enhanced and reaffirmed because that special form of ministry was there when she needed it. Her pastor could not fill the need himself, but could point her to another Christian resource in the community.

WARREN

Warren was devastated when he discovered that his wife had been having an affair. He had five children ranging from ten to seventeen, and he prided himself on being a family man. Now Helen was planning a "new life" for herself in a distant state, and the children were being asked to go with her.

Warren had recently enrolled in a Bethel Bible study, but under the circumstances he was tempted to drop the course. Fortunately, the pastor had built in a short time each week for sharing personal experiences and concerns. Since the group included only eight people, they had become well acquainted. When Warren shared his feelings of embarrassment, confusion, and guilt with the group, he was overwhelmed with the concern and support he received. The other members of the study encouraged him to stick with the course in spite of the extra load it entailed for him.

As the stressful months passed, the group learned a lot in addition to the regular curriculum. Close friendships developed that cemented Warren's Christian convictions and commitment to that congregation. His commitment to complete the course of study turned out to be an important key, representing stability amid a maze of changing personal circumstances.

Warren worked intently to help his church and others in the community cooperate on premarital education and training programs for engaged couples. In his case, a group that had other educational purposes was used to support and nourish him in a sensitive way. His commitment to Christ and the work of the church was strengthened because his pastor and the group were sensitive to individual needs as well as program goals.

Warren's Christian community was an effective part of his growth and healing process. They cared. They supported him when the rest of his world was collapsing all around him.

SUE

I remember calling my pastor, desperately needing someone to hear me. I had worked through much of my grieving, but I was still hurting a lot inside. I still had much bitterness to work through. He sent me to a counselor. We have a large congregation, and there's no way he could find enough hours for everybody. He was loving and helpful and had good resources at his fingertips.

So I went to a counselor, who at the end of our first session told me he didn't think I needed a counselor, just a friend. I explained that I was new in town and didn't really know anyone at church. My counselor became my friend. Sometimes I would weep through part of my session because I felt bankrupt in the feelings department. I had to give so much love and praise to my two babies, but nobody ever came home and said, "You're a good mommy." Nobody was there to kiss me when I hurt. And when I turned over at night, there was only cold and darkness.

I hurt so much, and Dr. Rey was willing to hear my pain. He heard my bitterness. He never judged me or preached to me telling me that God doesn't want us to hate those who hurt us. He let me express my emotions. He asked me about my children and how I was handling things. He told me I was a good mommy, that I was loving my kids, which was the most important thing. He reminded me that God had made me special and reflected some things that he saw in me that were really special. In short, he gave me some good strokes that I desperately needed.

Dr. Rey didn't psychoanalyze me. He let me share my grief and emotions. He encouraged me to be the special person God created me to be by helping me see where I was doing a good job under terrible adversity. I was still being a loving person. I continued to be sensitive after all my hurts. I hadn't put a wall around myself, and I was still willing to be vulnerable to others. He helped me rediscover that I was a worthwhile person.

GOOD LISTENERS

One way a faith community can respond in loving ministry is to have some people trained to listen. Perhaps your pastor is qualified to train listeners. Perhaps there is a psychologist or social worker in the congregation who would be willing to devote a few hours for a couple of listener training sessions. If not, perhaps the church could pay a

Christian psychologist for the needed training. Many congregations in larger populated areas contribute to Christian counseling centers where they can get counseling help at a reduced fee. The enabler training in chapter 7 might be another good approach to training good listeners. Some of these listeners could be "on call" for times of loneliness or crisis.

It is for each of us to minister to one another. Our pastors can't possibly minister to all the needs of everyone in their charge. The laity must take seriously the responsibility cited in Galatians 6:2 to "carry each other's burdens, and in this way . . . fulfill the law of Christ." A heavy burden can be lifted just in our listening to someone share his grief as he works through the pain of the past.

There may be a time when you can share your faith and hope as well. (The emphasis is on sharing, avoiding pontificating.) One effective way that we have discovered is to relate a common experience (if you have one) and then explain how God worked in that experience. For example, perhaps you have been through a divorce and can easily relate to many of the same situations the other person is now dealing with.

Or, perhaps you haven't been through a divorce, but you have had a hurting experience that you have learned to accept and overcome, such as a poor relationship with your father. You felt you were neglected by him and frequently verbally abused. You found yourself having love/hate feelings toward him. As years went by, your hostility grew into bitterness that ate at you constantly. One Sunday there was a sermon using Romans 12:14–21 as the text: "Bless those who persecute you; bless and do not curse. . . . Do not repay anyone evil for evil. . . . Do not take revenge, my friends, but leave room for God's wrath. . . . 'If your enemy is hungry, feed him; if he is thirsty, give him something to drink. In doing this, you will heap burning coals on his head.' Do not be overcome by evil, but overcome evil with good."

You had been praying about getting rid of your bitter feelings and now God, through a Sunday message, was telling you how to be free. Be kind to your father. Give up the hatred. Don't punish yourself with the burden of hostility. If your father needs punishing, God will handle it.

So when someone comes to you and says she's filled with bitterness toward her former spouse and is being eaten up with hatred, you can share your story with her. You can relate how you were once filled with bitterness and how you gave it up with God's help. Then you can write down for her where God's promise is found in Scripture so she can read and study it.

It is much more helpful for us to share the way God helped us than it is simply to quote Scripture at somebody. When hurting people can witness the living God at work in another person, they have truly been witnessed to by God's love and power. So when we share our hope and faith in the living God, we should do it through our own lives. Let God use our weakness as his strength.

PRACTICAL FRIENDSHIP

Sometimes listening and sharing our faith and hope isn't enough. We must also confirm God's will for us through good works. As it says in Hebrews 13:16, "And do not forget to do good and to share with others, for with such sacrifices God is pleased." If we know a divorced person who is a custodial parent with young children, we can anticipate many needs. If we live in a northern climate, winters are snowy. Perhaps if we have a hardy teenager or an energetic husband, we could call during a big storm and say, "As soon as we shovel out, we'll be right over." If we are older and have the shoveling done for us, we could offer to watch the little ones so the parent can go out and shovel for himself.

We might call one day and offer to watch the kids for a morning so Mom can have some quiet time at the grocery store or run some errands without hauling two little people in and out, fastening and unfastening car seats. We could send a postcard saying that the bearer is entitled to three hours of baby-sitting any Wednesday A.M. in March, twenty-four hours' notice requested.

Some noncustodial parents aren't interested in parenting. That leaves the custodial parents on twenty-four-hour call seven days a week. They probably work outside the home too. We can anticipate that most people would really appreciate a little time for themselves, knowing that some nice Christian family is watching their children, without the burden of another expense for their overextended budget.

If you live alone or your spouse travels a lot, perhaps you would enjoy some companionship. Chances are, there are some divorced people you know who would love some company. Perhaps you could go to a movie once a month together. Perhaps you could call somebody on the phone just to visit. You may want to ask them if you could pray for them. Ask them what their prayer needs are. You may find a common hobby: gourmet cooking, gin rummy, coin collecting, "garage saling"—something you could do together.

Perhaps you know an unemployed schoolteacher. She might enjoy teaching Sunday school. Reestablishing that part of her identity by using her talents can minister to her as she ministers to others. It also keeps people feeling they are a useful part of the body of Christ— that they can give as well as receive. Also, teaching Sunday school may help fill the gap of a noncustodial parent by letting him or her work with children. Encouraging a single person to host a meeting or some other event is another way the person can be encouraged to contribute.

MATERIAL ASSISTANCE

Sometimes material assistance may be called for, and there are many ways this can be handled. My pastor sent me to a psychologist. My church contributes to a Christian counseling center and paid most of my counseling fee. The center sees people on a sliding scale based on their income. I was unemployed and had no insurance, so I paid one-third of my reduced fee, and the church paid the rest. If the church hadn't been involved in a program like this, I would have missed a lot.

Another good way my church has found to provide material assistance is through a care-and-share pantry. The fourth Sunday of each month, the congregation is reminded to bring in canned goods, staples, or other items, which are collected in the narthex. These goods are moved into a pantry area and may be taken and used by people in need or distributed by the diaconal board when it hears of a need in the community.

The church supports counseling and other direct and indirect material assistance financially through a benevolence fund. Usually the first Sunday of the month is designated for benevolence giving. When the fund grows low in times of greater community need, the congregation is informed so they can prayerfully consider their benevolence giving.

In Hebrews 13:2 we are reminded how important hospitality is: "Do not forget to entertain strangers, for by so doing some people have entertained angels without knowing it." For the divorced, mealtime is just one more painful reminder of being alone. For the custodial parent, dinner is the beginning of second shift: It's coming home after a hard day's work to visit with the kids and get supper on the table. There's no one to share your day with. The kids are starved and crabby. And when you get the meal on the table, it's not time for you to eat, but rather to cut up food for the children. And if you don't have too many glasses of spilled milk, you may get a bite before everything's cold and the children have left the table.

For the noncustodial parent or divorced people without children, mealtime is when you read the paper while watching the news and eating something you really don't taste, because you just don't want to know you're eating alone again just as you do every other morning and every other evening. A nice way to minister to a divorced person is inviting him or her for a meal.

Sundays and holidays are even worse than regular mealtimes. Those are the traditional family times. Those are the days you feel the loneliest. On Sunday morning you sit alone in a family of believers. You see the loving glances of couples around you as they commune with the Lord. And you sit there feeling like an amputee. Half your being has been cut away, but unlike an amputee, no one can see your bloody stump.

Call someone who is divorced. Ask him to meet you in the narthex at 9:50, sit with your family, and come home with you for dinner after church.

Invite a divorcée and her two little children to your Fourth of July backyard picnic. It's a small gesture from you, but it can make a big difference to a lonely family.

These are just a few needs we can anticipate and minister to. We don't need to be psychologists, nor do we need to be rich. Just sensitive.

Calling someone and saying "If there's ever anything I can do" is usually a safe tactic, because most people will never call us back. If we really want to minister, we should think of a specific need. We can offer to mow the lawn or watch little ones while the divorced person mows it. Perhaps someone in the Christian community can repair a malfunctioning appliance, because many single-parent families just can't afford to buy a new one.

A good way to help divorced people feel welcome at church activities is not simply to say "all families welcome," but to make it clear that one-parent families and singles are meant by the term "families" also.

WOUNDED HEALERS

We have mentioned training listeners. Congregations today generally have a significant number of divorced members. Many of these have made healthy adjustments through difficult times and have made the important discovery that God was there strengthening them every step of the way. These people are especially valuable as trained listeners, since they will be able to empathize with many of the problem issues and will also share how God worked amid their weakness or pain.

For the person currently going through the pain of divorce, it is often helpful to see that others have survived the pain. It gives them hope that the Lord will sustain them and they will also survive.

Both my husband and I are survivors of divorce. We have had a singles Bible study in our home for two years. Initially it began with a couple of people in my Sunday school class wanting to get together during the week to share in the Word. We began fellowshiping together and now, instead of four people, there are twelve or fourteen. Only the early people get chairs, but nobody seems to mind. We get together and share our needs and strengths. We pray for one another. We study God's Word together. Sometimes we just get together for fun, knowing that God blesses even our just-for-fun times.

We haven't limited our group to the divorced. Several of our group are singles in their twenties. We have also invited a woman who was widowed several years ago to come and share in the fellowship. We let the group grow as it will, trusting God to bring to us those who need this ministry. Our pastor has channeled quite a few people into the group also. —Sue

Here is the key question we need to ask: "In fostering equipping ministries of various sorts, including evangelism, pastoral care, or teaching, can we focus upon the situation of divorce as an *opportunity* for healing ministry?" If the answer is yes, we should act on these ideas and develop even more.

As we each use our special gifts in ministering to others, let us remember the words of Christ from Matthew 25:35–40.

> " 'For I was hungry and you gave me something to eat, I was thirsty and you gave me something to drink, I was a stranger and you invited me in, I needed clothes and you clothed me, I was sick and you looked after me, I was in prison and you came to visit me.'
>
> "Then the righteous will answer him, 'Lord, when did we see you hungry and feed you, or thirsty and give you something to drink? When did we see you a stranger and invite you in, or needing clothes and clothe you? When did we see you sick or in prison and go to visit you?'
>
> "The King will reply, 'I tell you the truth, whatever you did for one of the least of these brothers of mine, you did for me.' "

3

EXPERIENCING GRIEF

I will never forget the moment when the doctor said to me, "I'm very sorry, your baby is dead." I shook my head slowly and said, "She can't *be dead. She* can't *be dead." I felt numb. It felt as if I was witnessing a terrible scene where a doctor was telling some poor woman that her beautiful little daughter was dead. I was outside looking at this horrible moment in someone's life. But it wasn't I. It couldn't be happening to me.*

Shock is probably one of God's least recognized gifts. I understood that a baby was dead, but I denied the possibility that she was my baby daughter. My daughter was going to grow up and take dancing lessons. I was going to cradle her in my arms and feel her soft, warm baby skin next to mine as she nursed at my breast. So it was nonsensical that someone would tell me all my dreams were over before they had a chance to begin. But my milk came in and no baby was brought to me. And soon the aching and throbbing of my breasts became the aching and throbbing of my heart, because reality was taking hold.

Grief filled my soul. I was trapped in an untenable situation. When I awoke the next day, everything wouldn't be the same as it was. Life would never be the same as it would have been. In one day my perspective changed.

—Sue

Divorce is a kind of death. It's the death of a relationship. It's the death of years of promise and promises. It's the death of years of planning. It's the death of love. It's the death of things shared. Who else remembers our son's first steps, stitches in the forehead on the Fourth of July, or walking in midnight air to help a baby with croup breathe more easily? Divorce is the death of a life together, rich with love and laughter, pain and hurt, and promises broken so completely that, like Humpty Dumpty, it seems that "all the king's horses and all the king's men" can't put that marriage together again.

23

Like death, divorce brings on that ritual of grief's emotional stages. The process usually usually starts with *shock and disbelief.* Those powerful feelings of "this can't be happening to me," like the feelings surrounding the death of a baby daughter.

For most people, the feelings of emptiness make reality hit fast and hard. "It did happen to me" comes crashing down like a brick wall. And we're left wondering in this lonely state—hurt, confused, and alone—whether it's even worth it to dig out of the rubble that continues to fall brick by brick with every ramification this new reality is foisting on us. We're left with intrusive, incongruous thoughts like "He left with the checkbook, all the bills are due next week, and I don't have a job." Or, "Why didn't I take the set of old dishes and the basement furniture before she had the locks changed?"

ANGER AND GUILT

No one seems surprised that *anger* and *guilt* emerge from a divorce situation. When the deep reality of the circumstances settles in, a person usually begins to search for who's to blame. The person who has chosen to initiate the divorce action will often feel a great deal of guilt. But there's enough guilt to go around for everyone to have a share.

Dan realized that he had been the dominant person in his marriage, and saw too late that he had hurt his wife, Jane, many times. Now that she seemed to be an emotional cripple, he felt he had probably wrecked her life, as well as his own and the children's too. That burden of responsibility kept him feeling guilty for most of the last year of his marriage, which was spent in separation. Dan and Jane continued to see a counselor weekly, but they made little or no progress.

Jane was convinced that no matter what changes or improved sensitivity Dan now seemed to display, she couldn't trust that his new behavior was genuine and not put on. She cautiously edged toward the decision to divorce. She didn't want to wreck his life, or his career, but it seemed she could never make her own decisions. She felt that to really be herself she needed to be free of his moody, domineering attitudes.

By the time Jane marshaled the courage to choose divorce, Dan realized he wasn't solely responsible for their failed marriage. His own counseling had begun to show him that her uncertainty and passivity had played directly into his tendency to make decisions, take charge, and have his own way. Now that she was finally going to give him the ultimate No, he felt powerless and really angry for the first time. He saw her as lacking the courage to go on with the marriage and work out their problems. His guilt was accompanied by anger when he realized that from now on he would be only a part-time father.

At the same time, as Jane approached the court date, her anger toward him for dominating her life was being replaced by deep guilt over her choice to "pull the plug" after all those years. Her family would never understand; they really liked Dan. And how could she earn an adequate living for herself and the children? The opinions of others contributed to her guilt feelings, but most of the blame was welling up from within herself. She was a deeply committed Christian. How could she have failed so miserably? Yet she was convinced the divorce had to come. She had to go through with it.

BARGAINING

Bargaining to salvage some part of the marriage usually will occur in a variety of ways. Sometimes people decide to have a truce with no hope of settling the conflict. A man who wants to keep his marriage intact may promise to get a better job, to go to church more often, to buy a new house, to stop drinking, to give up his friends, or the like. Sometimes these bargaining chips are slices of the real problems in the marriage. Sometimes they may be only strategies to avoid the real issues or to ward off the inevitable pain. Feelings associated with this unhappy time are anxiety, vigilance, and caution.

One may feel trapped, since the marriage does not seem to be capable of being repaired, yet no resolution or divorce settlement can be reached quickly. The fact that the marriage is over may be kept secret from the neighbors.

Bargaining over property and children inevitably ensues. But sometimes the bargaining becomes more like fighting. "If you don't stop bugging me, I'm going to see to it that you don't get a nickel! You're going to be in the poorhouse and the kids with you!" Impossible threats and fears surge back and forth. Both people may be struggling to hold on to what is truly dear to them, yet their efforts ironically damage them even more.

DEPRESSION

Depression is another step in the process of grieving. Donna was so depressed by her divorce that words of encouragement only caused her frustration. Donna's hair looked dirty. Her skin became pale, and she grew thinner. Her divorce support group met with her weekly for about two months before they all saw a change in her. She was beginning to show an interest in her appearance again. Her hair was clean and combed, and she was beginning to put on a little weight. Her group told her she was looking good. Their positive strokes overpowered her, however. She began to cry and said, "I don't want to make it. I want somebody to take care of me."

Donna's had a severe depression. She shared with her group that she weeps for days at a time. She is seeing a psychiatrist, who is helping her a great deal. Donna's attitude is changing and improving. Instead of saying, "I don't want to make it," she now says, "I know I can make it, I'm just not sure if I want to."

During some weeks Donna smiles and really feels as if she's doing better, but at other times she reports that she's had a bad week and is getting worse instead of improving. That's the moment when it's helpful to be reassured that relapses are normal. Grief is like that. We take five little steps forward and one big step backward. The trend is going the right way, but we have to be alert to setbacks.

Depression is not the same for everyone in feelings or intensity. For some, depression is feeling blue or lonely. For some it takes the form of despair and impotency, a feeling that nothing they can do will ever be enough to change their situation. They feel as if they are helpless victims of circumstance. Many will contemplate suicide. Some will attempt it, and a few of them will succeed. To them, the grief was so overwhelming that perspective got lost in pain. Jim Smoke expresses it well in his book *Growing Through Divorce:* "Divorce is one of the most painful and emotionally draining experiences that a human being can have. It is a hurt that goes deep and is accompanied by the doubt that it will ever heal."

ANGER-HOSTILITY

Another emotion of grieving is *anger-hostility.* "How could that rotten so-and-so do that to me? If that's how he wants it, I can get dirty too!" Anger and hostility often stir up feelings of hate and revenge. Sometimes anger is strong because we feel guilty in the breakdown of the relationship: If only I had or hadn't done something, everything would be all right. The guilt grows as we magnify the importance of an event or behavior, and the anger grows too. Often, the anger toward ourselves spills over onto someone else, and then our guilt, frustration, and anger begin growing again. People occasionally fantasize about how it would be if they got back together with their spouses, because the loneliness is closing in on them like the walls of a torture chamber in an old movie. The walls don't crush them, but the fantasy only increases the pain of their loneliness.

I read something in a diet book that reminded me of grieving. The author talked about the dieter's "yo-yo syndrome." A person will lose ten pounds, go off the diet, and gain back twelve. Then the dieter renews his dieting effort and loses twelve pounds. When he goes off the diet, he gains back fourteen.

Grieving is a yo-yo syndrome too. Sometimes you're up, sometimes you're down. Sometimes you're wound up tight, sometimes you're at the end of your rope. Sometimes your string gets frayed and needs a change, and sometimes the string even snaps. Grief comes and goes. It's a lot like yo-yos. —Sue

ACCEPTANCE

Finally, *acceptance* comes. Not only acceptance of the fact that we are divorced and alone, but also that each of us can make it as a single. After years of being identified as Abbott and Costello, the wonderful dynamic duo with a joint identity, somehow seen only functional as a unit, we discover that as Abbot alone we're a competent person. We can't do everything the same way we used to, but we can still make friends, laugh, work, cry, and have a full life with lots of relationships. Life isn't over. Only life with partner Costello is over.

For some people, particularly women, this may be the first time in their lives that they have carved out their own identity. There is an exhilaration in discovering that you can be a special person in charge of your own life. Mary said to her friends, "I'm so excited. I discovered I can decorate my new mobile home any way I want. I really can take care of the bills and the checkbook. I'm on my own for the first time, and I really can do it!"

As a wife and mother who didn't work outside the home, I will never forget the euphoric feeling of my first teaching job. Because I was in my thirties, my students figured I was a veteran teacher. My confident manner was never betrayed by my shaking knees of the first days, since they were hidden behind the podium. I was teaching in an inner-city school and had some tough kids, but after what I'd been through, I was strong, confident, and on top of the world.

I wish I could say this powerful façade never crumbled. And actually the façade didn't, but there were some days at the beginning of the semester when despair almost took over. I was frightened that I'd gotten in over my head. I imagined walking into the principal's office and telling him that I couldn't make it. I felt that this was really a turning point. If I couldn't handle this, would I ever be able to handle my life competently?

Well, I stuck with my tough kids and I didn't quit. The act of going through with something that acted out the principle that I was going to survive my divorce and all the emotional grieving that went with it became a symbolic act. It gave me confidence that I was a competent person. I had survived and was renewed. Acceptance brought peace.   —Sue

Acceptance is a sign of health and progress. But there's a lot that needs to be accepted, a lot being lost. The next chapter will focus on those elements of our lives that are lost with the end of a marriage. These "stations" along the way have potential for bringing on repeated echoes of the feelings of grief. Since they can repeat in unexpected cycles, they often add to confusion for both the divorced and those trying to help. But they can be understood.

4

PATTERNS OF LOSS AND GRIEF

Grief is stimulated by loss. Divorce is not just the loss of a mate. It is a group of losses, some unique to each individual, but many held in common among those who experience divorce. These losses are like losing a string of components that go together in making up the meaning of the marriage: a dream together, intimacy, companionship, parenting, material possessions, friends and family, a legal partnership, and a sense of "being one." One by one they slip away or lose their familiar shape. Each loss can be a frightening crisis, or many of them can come rushing in all at once like a personal earthquake, in which nothing seems to stand still.*

When we marry, each of us has a *dream*, a set of expectations that will result from our marriage. Common in this dream are things like happiness, companionship, sexual fulfillment, security, personal growth, and family. When divorce comes, we lose not only a mate, but these and hundreds of other dreams once shared.

Carl and Sandy worked hard. They bought and furnished a home and finally had two cars. Both Carl and Sandy were teachers, and for years they had dreamed of taking the children on a summer-long vacation. They would go to Niagara Falls, where they had spent their honeymoon. They would visit the college campus where they met. Three months is a long time, so over the years Carl and Sandy had spent hours talking to the children, brainstorming about all the places each person wanted to visit. When Carl and Sandy divorced,

---

*For a more clinical analysis of the loss and grief cycles, see "Making Sense of Divorce Grief," by Stanley Hagemeyer, in *Pastoral Psychology*, vol. 34, no. 4 (1986).

the years of saving, planning, and waiting for their big vacation, brought extra grief to everyone. The long-anticipated vacation dreams were lost too.

When most marriages begin, both partners find enjoyment doing things as a couple. They feel intimately bonded to one another. They join the young couples group at church. The young bride is willing to hold hands through a ball game she's not really interested in, and the new groom is willing to watch his exciting bride try on new dresses that both often understand they can't afford. What happens to that sweet *intimacy* of young love?

EMOTIONAL DISTANCE

When Joan got pregnant, her back ached. Sitting on wooden bleachers to watch her husband Jeff play softball didn't seem worth the little bit of companionship it brought. So she told Jeff to go to the games without her. Joan found herself alone quite often. Jeff had season football tickets and played racketball twice a week besides. So Joan signed up for some classes through a community education program. The only ceramics and painting classes she could get into were on nights that Jeff was home. But why should she be the one to give up everything?

Gradually Jeff and Joan felt greater emotional distancing. They both yearned for the intimate sharing they'd had. But resentment and anger sabotaged their feeble attempts at repairing the damage. They sometimes took opportunities to be away from each other just to show that they could get along without a companion. More and more time was spent apart, yet each of them sensed a hunger and a loss.

LOSS OF COMPANIONSHIP

A hollow, empty feeling would rise up when either of them heard someone speak of love and romance. Intimacy had been lost. They no longer really knew each other, nor took the time and energy to try to know. They weren't even available to each other most of the time. When Jeff moved out, it was a formalizing of something that had existed for quite a while. They led separate lives.

Yet, in spite of the obvious direction they had been following, this event brought feelings of grief to both of them. Each of them felt the loss of that companion they had known so well. The pain of that realization was almost too great to bear. They both yearned for what they had lost, but each grieved alone. Neither would admit to the other what they felt.

THE PARENTING ROLE

For couples with children, one parent has to give up the daily parenting role. Usually Dad is the one who just comes for visits, and he experiences his sense of loss repeatedly.

For Gerry, the loss of being a full-time father was the thing that finally brought out his anger. He had been calm and gentle but also guilty. Now he suddenly realized that his wife was going to take his children away from him. What did she know about raising two boys? How could she force him out of their lives? He was so angry at times he wished that she were dead: Maybe she would have a car accident. But his angry outbursts were also matched by lonely weeping. Often as he drove away from the family home on a Sunday night, just after delivering those precious little boys back to their mother, tears welled up in his eyes. With each visit he felt his loss once again.

For the custodial parent, the loss is different, but very real. That parent may fear the children won't be returned. Perhaps the other parent can't be trusted. Maybe they will have an auto accident. Sometimes in anger the noncustodial parent threatens to take the children by proving the other parent is somehow unfit. This fear haunts even the best custodial parents, since divorce brings strong feelings of insecurity.

If the noncustodial parent has moved out of state, the custodial parent may feel the extra burden of never having time off. With no partner to share the responsibilities, each daily task builds on the other to an overwhelming sense of never-ending responsibility.

FINANCIAL STRAIN

For most couples, divorce brings such a great financial strain that they are forced into losing a whole lifestyle as well. They learn to shop around at garage sales instead of just department stores, not just for their children's clothing, but even for furniture for the new apartment. The price of movies and baby-sitters are frequently prohibitive. So people who used to go out for dinner and a movie now stay home all the time.

But of even more consequence is the likelihood that one or both of the partners will lose the home and the car. Furnishings in the home must be divided up. One partner will even have to give up the beloved family pet.

For some, these losses are the easiest to take. For others, there is bitterness and feelings of being treated unfairly. The prestige of living in a nice home in a proper neighborhood may be very important. The embarrassment of affording only a cheap apartment or driving a rundown car may add to feelings of confusion about one's worth in the eyes of others. Our materialistic society places great value on what we own, and Christians seldom escape the impact of this value system completely. Just dividing up furniture or souvenirs can be a painful and unexpected occasion for renewed fighting, insults, or just quiet grief.

Many people who want to be fair and responsible go through much soul searching over their motives at this time.

THE LEGAL DIVORCE

For some, the legal formalities of filing, attending a hearing, and standing before a judge seem to have little impact. For others, the whole symbolic experience strikes with great force. There may be a high point of grief, or, in fact, a sense of great relief. For most, it seems, the final day of settlement does not pass without a sense of drama or stress. People may need special support at this time. In that case it's good for a close friend to accompany them.

LOSS OF COMMUNITY

The loss of property, although not a happy condition, is something people recognize ahead of time. Most people don't realize, however, that they will experience a loss of community. Some friends will take sides, remaining loyal to one partner or the other, while others will just stay away. Sometimes groups of couples will play bridge together for twenty years, but when a divorce occurs, neither of the partners will ever be included again. Perhaps some fear divorce may be somehow contagious and so think it wise just to keep their distance.

The last place we expect to find our community fading from us is church and family. Yet the couples club in which we've invested fifteen years building relationships just doesn't seem to know what to do with us as singles.

Our families? Often in their sense of loss or shock they seem to forget that we're so alone we feel as if we might not make it and we're not even sure if we care. So they visit sick friends and go to PTA meetings and think they'll call us sometime . . . and months and sometimes years slip by. The loss of community—friends, church, and family—often entails a set of unexpected and very painful losses.

LOSS OF PERSONAL IDENTITY

The concept of two becoming one flesh can get mixed up in a marriage so that sometimes one partner relates too strongly with the identity of the other. Then, when divorce comes, it means that one partner *loses personal identity*. Clara was an honor student in high school. She was an excellent seamstress, gourmet cook, and budget balancer. She had many abilities and talents. Her husband George was bullish and undermined each thing Clara did. After thirty years of marriage, Clara goes to George for directions on the littlest detail. She no longer feels sufficient self-worth to make even a simple decision.

Divorce is earth-shattering for someone like Clara, since divorce actually removes the decision maker from her life while leaving her self-image crippled. Through the years she has learned to see herself not as her own person but somehow as an appendage of her husband, his status, his identity. For her and others like her, loss of marriage is loss of identity. There will be much grieving and painful growing before she can realize she is a separate person and a significant one in her own right.

Another identity problem frequently occurs when a divorce takes place—as it often does—about the time that the last children flee the nest. The mother may be experiencing a mid-life crisis. She may have invested more of her energy into being a good mother than into being a good wife. Now she feels useless, not needed by either her children or her husband.

Most researchers emphasize the need for people to reestablish their identity after a divorce, but letting go of their identity with their past partner is not easy. Some "feel married" for years after their spouse has left. Others experiment with new and bizarre behaviors, which surprise even their friends, but they finally settle down again a year or two later. All the components of "who I am" are up for review, even those that are not intrinsic to the marriage. Some change jobs and adopt new hobbies or habits. The more the church and community can stand by to provide a reliable set of friends who are not changing, the more stable a person is able to feel.

UNDERSTANDING CONFUSING PATTERNS

The literature regarding patterns of divorce recovery reveals a confusing array of experiences. Some people seem to experience shock, denial, and the other stages of grief over and over again.

Others experience them in varying sequences. The patterns are similar, but confusing. They can best be explained as a combination of stages of grief together with a succession of losses:

Each of the losses—the marriage dream, intimacy, companionship, parenting, property, friends, and so on—has the potential for setting in motion the stages of grief once again. The waves of shock, anger, bargaining, depression, and acceptance may appear repeatedly. Some stages will seem more prominent than others. However, each succeeding loss delivers an impact that may restart the process of grieving.

Friends or counselors working with the person may be surprised that they have "gone back" to being angry again, after a time of acceptance or resolution.

It would seem to me that what is happening is that each new realization being lost in the marriage is like a pebble dropped into a pool of water. A wave of emotions is set off again and again, perhaps reinforcing waves already in motion, enhancing their depth, or adding new ripples to an already confusing pattern of disturbance. Some pebbles are bigger, some smaller. The pool is seldom quiet.

—Stan

After leaving home, for example, the husband immediately grieves for his children and his active role in fathering them. Within about six months, he has worked through his grieving to acceptance and is really feeling as if life is looking up. He and his former spouse have worked out a liberal visitation schedule, and he is actually spending more quality time with the children than he did when he was home.

Just as he begins to feel good about life again, the financial crunch hits hard. He realizes he will have to sell some property and trade his lovely little Boston Whaler for a rowboat if he wants to continue to fish. Denial and anger reappear. So for each loss, as we experience it, we begin grieving. And we work through these stages of grief—at different speeds, depending on how great each loss was for us.

Sometimes we get stalled on an emotional stage during our grieving process. To Karen, financial matters were a high priority. When she and John went through their divorce, Karen grieved over the loss of her large home and her housekeeper. Two years later, Karen is still angry. She hasn't been willing to accept the financial burden her divorce placed on her. She has worked through her emotional stages of grieving quite well in other respects, however. For some, acceptance seems like defeat instead of starting over, and these people remain stuck in a quagmire of bitter feelings—unwilling to accept, unable to grow.

Whatever we value the most, we will grieve for the most. For Karen, accepting financial backsliding was especially difficult because that was such a high priority for her. Each loss of role we experience deepens the feelings of lost identity. Noncustodial parents lose that parenting part of their identity. Those who must sell their homes lose the identity of homeowner. For those who derived most of their identity from their marriage partner, the loss is even more severe. They go through a period much like early adolescence, wondering "Who am I?"

All those who must give up part of their identity must do some self-discovery to fill the empty spaces left in their lives. This is crucial to develop autonomy. The divorced must work hard to find out who they are now. They must determine what they will do today and tomorrow to take charge of their own lives, and to take responsibility for the future.

SUCCESSIVE LOSSES AND CYCLICAL EMOTIONAL STAGES

Losses may set off the emotional stages repeatedly.
These can cause various overlapping patterns which
have the appearance of being cyclical.

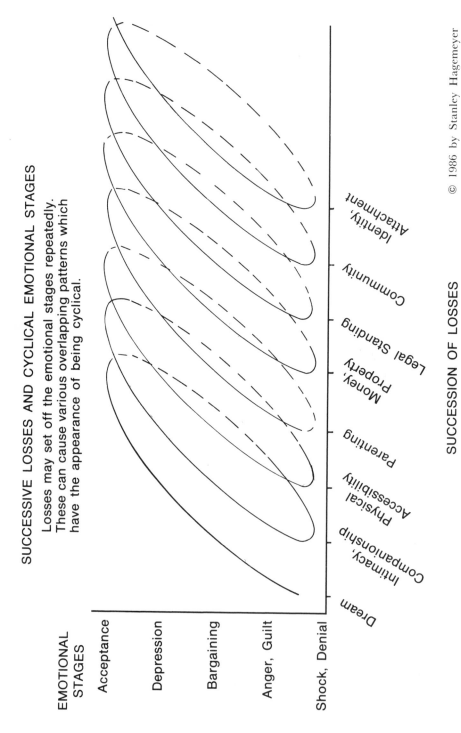

EMOTIONAL STAGES

Acceptance

Depression

Bargaining

Anger, Guilt

Shock, Denial

Dream

Intimacy, Companionship

Physical Accessibility

Parenting

Money, Property

Legal Standing

Community

Identity, Attachment

SUCCESSION OF LOSSES

5

EVALUATING THE CHOICES FOR MINISTRY

It is important to look at some different types of ministry to the divorced and then to consider our own needs in order to evaluate which type of ministry is the most appropriate for our congregation.

MINISTRY SUPPORT TEAM

One kind of outreach is the ministry support team, which has the specific, defined objective of befriending the divorced and separated. Identify people in the congregation who are especially suited to serve as resources to the pastor in befriending the separated or divorced. Look to those previously divorced—including those who have remarried—and family members of divorced people who were good supporters and who seem to have weathered their family experiences positively.

Bring together those who are willing to get involved for a brief orientation session to ask them to be available to do some sharing and perhaps to be on call. Often knowing that there is someone who is willing to listen means a great deal to a person under stress. Volunteers will need some training in good listening skills (see ch. 7). You should remind volunteeers that they are not there to solve problems, but to be sensitive listeners. The hurting people will be going through the stages of grieving discussed in chapter 3. There could be a lot of raw emotions expressed, and the listeners should be prepared to cope with these and help the hurting person cope also.

Listeners should help to identify emotions and reflect back to the speaker (see ch. 7 for an explanation of this). The person experiencing divorce needs to feel understood. However, because God's commands are always intended for our good, the listener can confront violations of biblical standards. And always remember that confidentiality must be strictly maintained. The ministry support team should read or be coached on chapter 2, "Needs the Church Can Meet." This will be very helpful to them.

The support team should meet monthly for sharing and for supporting one another. If the support team is expected to remain a permanent part of the church's ministry, this meeting of sharing and visiting is crucial. It fosters a sense of unity and encouragement. It may be desirable to have prayer partners within the team so that if a problem arises they can call on each other for prayer support. There should also be a resource person whom the team members can consult as an expert if a situation should arise that they don't know how to handle; this could be the pastor, a church officer, or perhaps a psychologist in the congregation.

SINGLES SUNDAY SCHOOL CLASS

Another approach to ministry is to provide a small-group education/support class in the Sunday school. Offer an elective for the divorced and separated with an appealing title like "Resingled" or "S.T.I.C.S." (Singles Together in Christ) or "Living Alone as a Single Christian." The leader should be someone in the congregation who has survived divorce and has shown spiritual growth from that painful experience.

Because divorce is a time of emotional upheaval, it is important for the divorced to feel that the church has a special place for them. It can be awkward to attend a couples' class as a new single, so having the option of a class for the divorced and separated is a gesture recognizing the hurt and special need for ministry.

A class such as this serves as a support group. It gives people the opportunity to understand that they are not the only divorced Christians in the world and, more importantly, that because others have survived, they can too. It gives people with a common root—Christianity—and a common problem—divorce—the opportunity to nurture one another as they grow. The class can demonstrate the truth that God uses times of pain to bring each of us closer to him.

There are many excellent books with a scriptural basis that are suited for use in a singles' class. They may be especially for singles or just topically relevant, such as books on suffering, pain, or loneliness. A study of the Twenty-third Psalm is appropriate at this time, and there are some good study books that deal with the psalm.

The extensive bibliography at the back of this book contains a wide range of good publications from which to select ones appropriate to your class. A local Christian bookstore and the magazines and newsletters listed in the bibliography are sources of additional information. A bulk subscription to a singles magazine such as *Spirit* can offer continuing encouragement for your class and may sometimes provide useful discussion materials also.

Again, do not fail to recognize the importance of training. A class or any other context for singles to meet must be led by someone who is able to foster frank and free discussion. Look for leaders who can be trained, and then provide the training. A suggested approach to training is offered in chapter 7.

SMALL SUPPORT GROUPS

The third type of ministry to consider is a small group for separated and divorced people outside the Sunday morning church schedule. This can open up the group to participation from those who may attend other churches and is more likely to attract support from other pastors. The location of a seminar is discussed in chapter 6; it suffices to say here that there can be advantages in meeting somewhere besides in a church building.

A good choice for leadership in this kind of group is a couple whose partners have experienced divorce and second marriage. This gives the Bible study some continuity, since singles' classes have a high turnover rate. The couple is a steadying influence to the group, and their authority will be accepted because of their experiences. Chapter 7 discusses finding and training leaders.

The variety of good materials listed in the bibliography is a starting point for selecting resources. One means of reaching a decision is to purchase a few of the items and distribute them to several potential seminar participants or leaders for review. Then hold a meeting at which the publications can be discussed and a group decision made.

Another possibility is a Bible study, using a discussion format rather than a lecture. Many of the Psalms are rich resources for such occasions, because they deal with feelings and relationships.

A small-group meeting should last one-and-a-half or two hours. There should be a good balance between Bible study and sharing times. Time for sharing personal concerns that are not directly related to the subject matter being studied is essential to make sure the group members are in touch with each other on personal needs.

Don't get bogged down in covering the study material so that people are discouraged from sharing; but provide enough guidance that the group doesn't just drift through trivia all evening.

When a person enters the group as a newcomer, introductions can be made in entertaining ways. For example, one person introduces another member of the group by telling a story about that person. That person in turn chooses another to tell something about. This means of introduction is a good icebreaker, a relaxed and heartwarming way to meet a group.

As people arrive, it is good to chat over a cup of coffee and find out how their week went. When everyone is present and the refreshments are finished, the study can begin. A topical study on pain, loneliness, or trial can lead to helpful personal sharing and growth. If a couple of Bible truths can be brought out, understood, and applied, and if the group has time to relate personal testimonies, hardships, and prayer needs, the group is standing on God's words and bearing one another's burdens.

A newsletter can be an entertaining way to extend fellowship during the week for either a Sunday school class or a Bible study group. The next week's assignment can be listed along with any good kernels of biblical truth that have been brought out during study times. There can be a joke section and other creative content contributed by members. The newsletter helps keep people in touch who miss a meeting and reminds those who are having a difficult week that fellowship and support are near at hand.

Having prayer partners is also a good idea. A commitment for each pair to contact one another at least once during the week provides a meaningful means of emotional support.

Another possibility is a cooperative effort with other churches. Perhaps several churches in a geographic area could do a little preliminary, cooperative planning to arrange time, location, leaders, and materials. The meeting place could be set up on a rotating basis every eight weeks, every quarter, or every season. Again, it is important to build in sharing time and prayer time. Some professional leadership may be helpful, but as soon as possible this cooperative group ought to be granted autonomy. The participants can then set their own agenda and choose their own materials. Crossing denominational and sociological boundaries will bring vitality and richness to any program.

This small-group approach can be used in a specialized group mainly for those newly divorced or separated. In that case, the seminar outline in chapter 6 is helpful, following the material in Jim Smoke's book *Growing through Divorce.* Other useful books are listed along with this one in the annotated bibliography.

LARGE SUPPORT GROUP

Meetings that are widely publicized and open to drop-in visitors each week can offer an attractive format for a community-wide ministry. People will often feel free to visit if meetings are held in a neutral, nonchurch setting. One program we have worked with was so successful that we soon had requests for groups from other parts of our community, and this led to holding several meetings weekly, using different facilities. These were simply called "Creative Growth" meetings, and the topics we publicized indicated it was primarily for single adults.

Ideally a group like this has a regular meeting place, which may or may not be a church building. A typical agenda for a meeting is for the chairperson to give announcements—that is, tell the topic for next week's meeting and introduce the speaker for the evening. The speaker talks on the given topic for about an hour. Then the participants are assigned to small discussion groups, to which they disperse after a fifteen-minute coffee break. In these groups the people discuss questions that have been provided by the speaker. The formal meeting lasts just two hours, but it could be followed by casual socializing at a nearby coffee shop.

A key ingredient to success is having a corps of leader volunteers present at every meeting who have been trained as "enablers," or small-group leaders (see ch. 7). They are assigned to lead the small groups during the second hour and serve as facilitators to make these discussions productive and supportive for each participant.

A group like this should be structured to have one person ultimately responsible for three committee leaders. Committee one is in charge of refreshments. This committee is responsible to see that light refreshments—such as beverages and cookies—are provided by themselves or others. Committee two is responsible to sign up speakers on preselected topics and to call the speaker a week before the speaking engagement to remind him of his commitment. Committee three is responsible for publicity. It contacts local radio stations and newspapers for public-service announcements of local events. It would also be responsible to oversee the group newsletter if there is a volunteer editor and if funds are available for mailing (see appendix A).

These four people—the overall leader and the three committee leaders—should plan the programming as a group. They may wish to glean ideas from the other participants and recruit regular attenders to share the responsibilities.

Speakers are usually abundant in metropolitan areas. Christian psychologists, divorced clergy, and Christian laypeople with good speaking skills who have survived divorce are all potential speakers. Good films are another helpful source.

The following is a list of some of the topics that could be included in a group program:

Learning to Recognize Feelings
Emotional Needs of Children
Divorce, Dating, and Remarriage: What the Bible Says
Experiencing Loss Through Death and Divorce
Changing Jobs, or Getting Back Into the Job Market
Stress Management
Where to Go for Help: Car, Home, Appliance Repairs, Etc.
Self-Defeating Behavior
Sexuality and the Single Life
Effective Communication
Financial Affairs
Self-Love and Self-Esteem
Single by Choice
Wholeness as a Single Person
Tips on Mental Health
Overcoming Loneliness During Holidays
Coping
Dealing With Guilt
Alcoholism and Its Ramifications
Choosing a Mate: The Ghost of a Marriage Past
Mid-Life Crisis

One of the natural difficulties that develops in a group like this is a concern to meet the needs of the newly single while also serving those who have been single for a longer time. If this tension is kept in balance, both kinds of people can continue to attend and feel the group is really for them.

It is highly advisable that to deal with this problem, a new small group, as described earlier above, be offered several times a year just for the newly separated or divorced. Then the larger group meetings can be an ongoing series attuned to the broader interests of single adults. In this way the newly single people can move from the smaller group into the larger one whenever they feel ready to do so, or they may attend both simultaneously.

A newsletter becomes a vital part of this ministry because it will communicate the schedule of forthcoming topics, in a way, it is hoped, that attracts new people as well as regular attenders. The newsletter also gives the group a sense of identity and special belonging within the church or larger community. Names and phone numbers of leaders enable people to keep in touch. The newsletter or smaller versions of the schedule of topics can be given to newcomers and posted on bulletin boards at the participants' places of work. Similarly, a business card could be printed that lists the group's name and meeting place and a phone number for information; this can be used to inform and recruit others for the group.

DIVORCE MINISTRY SEMINARS

The fourth type of ministry to consider is a seminar that helps the divorced cope with their new lives. Stan has done a great deal of research and has led a comprehensive divorce ministry in a major city. His experience can prove helpful in launching a successful community-wide ministry. Chapter 6 introduces the concept of a seminar that takes place over several weeks in contrast to a one-day event. The chapter offers guidance for planning, training personnel, arranging lectures, and tending to other details of conducting community-wide seminars on coping with divorce.

MAKING A DECISION

How can we determine which approach to ministry is called for in our congregation and community? We suggest that the following questions be answered before a decision is made:

1. How many separated/divorced people live within a twenty-minute drive of the church?

2. How many divorces are granted each year within that area? Multiply by two to know how many hurting people there are.

3. How many separated/divorced people are in our congregation at any one time? When a divorce occurs, we will have only a few months to meet the need, because one or both parties will likely leave the church within a year.

4. Is the church committed to ministry to the whole person? Are we concerned with physical, emotional, and financial needs?

5. Would the church rather delegate ministry for the divorced to a specialized agency outside the congregation? The answer "yes" does not necessarily mean there is dereliction of duty, for no church has the resources to meet *every* human need.

6. Are the ministries of the church already taking account of or already involved in various kinds of outreach that express God's love—programs such as the distribution of clothing or money, a food pantry for the hungry, hospitality for the needy during holidays? How many of these can be adapted to the needs that accompany separation/divorce?

7. What other churches or church leaders in the area are sensitive to these issues and could be contacted to develop a cooperative ministry?

8. What existing agencies or community groups may be interested and could support the values we hold—such as the YMCA, the YWCA, and ecumenical associations? What local employers or businesses might be willing to support our efforts financially, print brochures, etc.?

9. How much money are we willing to commit to a year's experiment in this ministry? How does this commitment compare with that of other programs?

10. What outside resources might we turn to to launch the program? Are there singles ministry professionals, counselors, or volunteers in nearby towns?

11. What programs are operating within an hour's drive that we could visit to observe and gather information, ideas, or encouragement? Who are potential leaders that might make such a visit? Are there national or regional events they could attend for inspiration and ideas?

While you and your friends are carefully considering these questions, you will probably find your enthusiasm building. There *is* opportunity for ministry. You simply need to decide how you are going to do it, and then get started.

PART II

6

THE COPING WITH DIVORCE SEMINAR

Seminars are now being conducted in a variety of ways. Our research shows that one of the most popular is a weekend experience. This kind of event can often attract a wide audience if it is well promoted or it features a well-known main speaker. The intensive time available on a weekend can be very helpful. A participant may leave the event feeling stimulated and hopeful; much team spirit can be developed; and new friendships may flourish.

But too frequently there is a letdown feeling when a weekend seminar is over. The new acquaintances go their own way, and the seminar becomes just a pleasant memory. Because the event is an intense experience in a compact time frame, there is little chance of behavior modification. Ideas are planted, but stimulation for further growth is unavailable and the opportunities for long-term growth are diminished.

Another kind of seminar takes place over a period of weeks. In this seminar, the participants meet for a number of weekly sessions of perhaps two hours duration. Although participants don't have the same opportunity to bond quickly with one another, the bonding will come in time. And the time-separated seminar has the advantage of working on a new skill or aspect of the person each week, giving participants the opportunity to be regularly accountable to their colleagues on their progress or lack of it. Over a period of perhaps eight weeks, participants will watch themselves grow while being encouraged as they encourage others.

Another option is to combine these two formats by beginning a multiweek seminar with a weekend kickoff. By using this option, there are many obvious advantages, although this may make the price prohibitive to many if accommodations prove costly.

EVALUATING EFFECTIVENESS

We suggest six criteria for evaluating the effectiveness of seminars. They will be helpful in our understanding of what makes a seminar for divorced people effective.

1. Does the program provide *information* to educate participants concerning the emotional stages, losses, and tasks that accompany separation and divorce?

2. Does the program provide for the development of *coping skills* to assist participants in assessing their resources in response to the challenges and stress of divorce?

3. Does the program promote a safe and accepting atmosphere where *emotions* can be *expressed, faced, and accepted* by the participants?

4. Does the program provide for *personal growth* that includes the dynamics of self-examination, confession, forgiveness, and renewal within either a psychological or religious framework?

5. Does the program prepare a person for *re-socializing?*

6. Does the program call for the effective use of *small groups* with trained leaders for the purposes that are addressed in criteria 1 through 5?

The seminars we plan should meet these six criteria. The seminar described in the second part of this book does so. It is based on the Coping With Divorce seminars conducted by the Good News Community of Grand Rapids, Michigan. These seminars have ministered to more than three thousand people over the course of several years. They have been tried and have proved to be a very positive outreach ministry.

CHOOSING A LOCATION

One crucial factor that has surfaced from experience is location. Some groups have been trained and have transplanted the Coping With Divorce seminars into other cities near Grand Rapids. One group decided to hold the seminar in a church building; another chose the community building of an apartment complex. The latter met with considerable success and eventually formed its own nonprofit corporation. The one that started out in a church building has been unable to grow or gain momentum.

After a divorce, people are often hesitant to attend their own churches, let alone a strange church. They may fear someone will begin preaching a moralistic message that is insensitive to their bruised emotions. Also, by meeting in a "neutral zone," our evangelistic outreach will actually be increased by attracting both Christians who may be alienated from their own churches and nonbelievers who are hurting people searching for answers and someone to share their burdens with. A neutral site is a facility such as a high school auditorium, a community education building, a library, a town hall, a community building, or a local business cafeteria.

Look for a building that will avoid excuses for people. There should be plenty of free parking space available. The meeting room should seem cozy, but not lounge-like. Carpeting and drapes encourage a cozy atmosphere and also help to make the environment quieter. The room must be large enough to hold fifty to sixty people without crowding and must also allow for dispersing into small groups. If it is possible, some additional small rooms adjacent to the lecture hall may be useful for the small-group sessions.

Fellowship is encouraged by a little coziness. Movable chairs are necessary to move into a circle at group time. They also promote a more businesslike feeling than do overstuffed chairs. Some people will prefer having small groups around tables because they feel emotionally "safer." Others don't like to be around tables, feeling it creates a sense of distance. The person in charge of facilities should be aware of these differences when looking over the options.

Whatever location is selected, it should be well marked. The exterior of the building should have the proper entrances marked. The interior should have arrows directing people to the proper room.

Kurt, a community education teacher for several years, greatly appreciated the greeting he received at the seminar he attended in Grand Rapids. He struggled with the decision of whether or not to attend and put off attending for a year; he didn't want to admit that he had problems dealing with his new lifestyle after his divorce. He finally reached the parking lot. Any excuse would have sent him the other way, but he saw the seminar signs and felt a little encouragement. When he entered the building, some volunteers greeted him at the door with welcoming smiles and invited him to follow the signs. Kurt was encouraged to follow through with the seminar. He told this story the last week of his seminar. He was very thankful he had come and had been ministered to. He was also thankful for the signs and the volunteers who gave him the courage to begin.

COMMUNITY COOPERATION

As we begin to map out our seminar strategy, we must not forget to seek community cooperation. Personal visits to labor union officials, people in substance abuse programs, personnel offices, counseling centers, and legal centers will be beneficial. These are people who come in contact with large numbers of divorced people who may be wondering where they can turn for information and support. Paying visits to these people lays important groundwork for mailing seminar brochures and public awareness of the integrity of our organization. Without the personal visit the brochures might be met by skepticism and disinterest; instead, the progam has already been introduced before the brochures are mailed. When people come to these agencies for help, they will likely be given a brochure and informed of the seminar.

These agencies must understand that our purpose is to help people. Only secondarily should it be mentioned that the seminar is a form of evangelism. If it is seen as a service program, people will want to take part. The evangelistic benefit must be seen as the church and Christians showing the community that they have integrity, that they have their interests at heart, and that they care about people. Then they become credible. The quiet and effective ministry comes when people ask, "How did you survive divorce?" Questions like these give the leaders many opportunities to share the variety of ways that God has helped them and how the grace of God has worked through others to give them new hope and strength. This personal witness and encounter is much more effective than a speaker preaching to hurt and angry people, simply telling them their needs will be met by Christ.

There are always many people in positions of influence delighted to find an organization with good Christian values to which they can refer people. You will find that these visits will be well worth the hours of volunteer time they require.

BASIC IDEAS FOR PLANNING

We recommend an eight-week seminar of two hours per week. The format calls for a lecture of approximately forty-five-to-fifty minutes, a fifteen-minute coffee break, and fifty-five-to-sixty minutes in small-group discussions. It is beneficial to suggest a common meeting place—such a pizza place or coffee shop—where people can socialize after the seminar session is over.

Here is an outline of choices to consider in planning a seminar:

1. Plan a full-blown cooperative effort, including the seminar and support meetings.
   a. Study various designs for larger seminars, and recruit other churches to help design and promote the program.
   b. Recruit potential leaders (divorced Christians) from a wide variety of churches, suggested by their pastors.
   c. Carry out a full preparation/publicity program using methods suggested by us or other materials.
   d. Once a successful series has been carried out, expect the cream to rise to the top. Potential leaders for carrying on to the next step will appear from within the ranks.
   e. Plan to repeat the major program once or twice a year, or more frequently if called for, with less structured activities in between.

A large church with strong financial and personnel resources may choose to carry out the whole program on its own. Attendance at these meetings will not be promoted or encouraged very well by other church leaders, unless clear attempts are made to defuse any sense of competition or "losing" their members.

2. Encourage development of a seminar/class within already existing agencies.
   a. Local community education departments, community colleges, and the like can promote classes to touch practical needs if they are given suggestions about resource people and materials to use.
   b. Nonprofit groups like the YWCA, YMCA, family service associations, government agencies, Friend of the Court, and ecumenical ministerial associations will respond if enough citizens or groups ask for this community service.

While these may not seem to be "Christian" in sufficient depth to represent the church's goals, they do represent an opportunity for incarnational ministry. *Usually* there are Christians working in these agencies who can be given a chance to minister within their work arena. In addition, volunteers will still be necessary to make the program function. Encouraging Christian singles to get involved provides the opportunity for them to witness in quiet, practical ways such as leading small groups and instilling values into an otherwise "secular" program.

3. Encourage the development of an autonomous "transition support organization" in your city or community, similar to the YMCA or Alcoholics Anonymous. Call it Community Singles, Singles Together in Christ, or something similar.
   a. Help the group to launch programs and encourage an ecumenical basis to provide some promotion and support but give them autonomy.
   b. Trust singles, separated, and divorced people to know what the needs are and to make decisions about their own special form of ministry.

This strategy can be incorporated into the ministry of a large, well-rounded congregation, especially one willing to commit a strong budget and a staff member to supervise the program.

When I first attempted to arrange a Coping With Divorce Seminar, I asked a number of pastors to suggest divorced people in their congregations who might be interested in serving as volunteers in this special ministry.

I was amazed at the quality of the volunteers who came forward. Many churches had intelligent, committed Christians in them who were just waiting for an opportunity to serve in this special way. Since they had each suffered through many agonizing experiences, God's love motivated them to want to help make such experiences less painful for others. They were willing to make commitments to the required training in preparation for the seminar as well as the weeks of meetings that followed. They all had a genuine concern for others that impressed participants and stimulated many of them in turn to volunteer to help with all aspects of the program as it was repeated in months and years to follow.

—Stan

Part 2 of this book is a how-to manual for planning and conducting a Coping With Divorce Seminar. Chapter 7 deals with recruiting and training volunteers. Chapter 8, "What You Need to Start," has information on responsibilities that need to be fulfilled before the seminar begins, such as funding and how to schedule preparation tasks.

Chapter 9, "Handouts," contains several handouts including evaluation forms on enablers, the seminar, and participants, along with an explanation of why these are helpful. There is also a handout to show how to make a local singles resource list.

Chapter 10, "Leaders' Notes and Seminar Materials," provides the information the emcee of the seminar needs to present to the participants each week. Chapter 11, "Seminar Topics," suggests the general content of each weekly session.

Appendix A, "Promoting and Publicizing the Seminar," covers information on printing brochures, scheduling advertising, and planning other publicity.

The bibliography is an excellent resource that should be made available to all the participants. If possible, it is good to have a book table at the seminar location the second week and thereafter. A volunteer can tend the table, which should display a number of the books listed in the bibliography.

YOUR OPPORTUNITY

The tools are here for you to begin a creative divorce ministry. If you want to get started in a creative ministry of healing for those who hurt, providing friendship to the lonely and guidance for the searching, the following chapters will help. Creative divorce ministry is a process of applying in original ways the principles and tools that are available for our own circumstances, town, and people.

God often uses ordinary people to bring about extraordinary results. People who become involved as leaders will enjoy the satisfaction and surprising delight that they can minister in ways that touch deeply. Whichever strategy or methods we choose, we can have an impact on individuals that they will never forget. Our society's woes and individual tragedy are like the rich ground where the seed of grace, acceptance, and renewal can be planted with great success.

7

RECRUITING AND TRAINING ENABLERS

One person who understands the principles of leadership and sharing is not enough for a successful seminar. This chapter explains the steps required for recruiting and training small-group leaders, whom we will call "enablers." The method of having many take part in the process of healing/sharing is consistent with the biblical principle of the Body of Christ having many parts, each with a distinct function. This expression of the priesthood of believers is an essential and effective ingredient of ministry.

The Role of Enablers

Enablers are volunteers who have experienced separation or divorce and have been trained in listening skills and group leadership. They serve as small-group leaders, fulfill other seminar leadership and organizational roles, and are also available as a contact to provide listening and support within the limits of their time and ability.

Their main purpose is to enable seminar participants to discover and exercise their own abilities and to take responsibility for themselves. Enablers are not expected to solve problems or give answers to participants. They function more as encouraging role models who take a special interest in other people and assist them in reentry into the single life.

Recruiting a Team

1. Talk to local pastors. Find out who has been divorced and may be likely to want to help others. Then ask those you are

guided to if they would be willing to help and if they would like to be trained to help others.

2. Here are qualities to look for in good enabler candidates:
   a. Do they care about others? Is their motivation to help others or do they just want to meet a new spouse?
   b. Can they be trained to do more listening than they do talking or teaching?
   c. Do they have to be experts? No, just peers.
   d. Must they be mature Christians? No, but they need to be committed to Christ and willing to serve. A person who is highly educated in doctrine will not necessarily have the communication skills needed for dealing with people in these kinds of situations.
   e. They must be flexible. Pat answers are not helpful.
   f. They must be willing to commit themselves to the established number of training sessions and seminar meetings. If they are willing to help but can't make an extended time commitment, it might be good to recruit them for another job in the program that requires less time, such as making name tags or helping with publicity.

TRAINING GOALS

The primary concern in training is not the learning of ideas, but rather the learning of behaviors or skills. How the enablers act during the small-group meetings will determine to a large degree the success of the program as a whole. Their purpose is to be a supportive part of a small group of people who care about one another. Therefore the attitude of enabler volunteers is crucial, and their ability to perform well will depend on whether they can demonstrate a quiet, caring attitude without needing to assert their opinions.

These are the goals to be accomplished during the training:

1. Build a sense of team commitment and anticipation.
2. Develop effective listening skills.
3. Build small-group management skills.
4. Gain an overview of the total seminar and its purpose.
5. Give enablers an opportunity to practice sharing their own experiences.

SELECTING A TRAINER

Unfortunately, many of us have received very little preparation or instruction in the task of training others. If the pastor or some other church leader has received training in counseling or small-group development, he or she may be just the one to take the responsibility. However, it may be good to recruit a Christian from outside the church in the field of education, mental health, or a similar profession who can contribute the time and expertise to accomplish the training, regardless of whether or not the person intends to help lead the seminar.

There are many dedicated Christians in these fields who would enjoy the opportunity to be involved. Don't hesitate to ask for help. These people would also be helpful in planning the details of the training and make improvements to fit the local circumstances.

The training program that follows is intended for people who have not been previously trained, but it may be adapted for use with enabler candidates with previous experience.

FIRST TRAINING SESSION*

The trainer should allow two to two-and-a-half hours for each of the three sessions. The material can be used in two sessions of three hours each, or a more intensive weekend schedule, but the extended time of three weeks is recommended to give trainees more time to assimilate and practice what they are learning. An approximate time schedule is provided to help guide the trainer. He should have a list of the volunteers attending the meetings and use name tags at each session.

OBJECTIVES
1. Group building, heightening expectations, team spirit
2. Initial practice in honest, vulnerable sharing
3. Overview of the seminar and understanding of each week's specific purpose

Time Activity

7:30   *Introduction.* Welcome the group and state the purpose of the training sessions in preparation for the seminar. Emphasize the importance of attending all the training sessions.

---

*This training program is adapted from "The Enabler Training Plan," copyright © 1985 by the Good News Community, Inc., Grand Rapids, Michigan. Used by permission.

7:40   *Total Group Sharing.* Ask the group to respond to the following, allowing time for each person to respond before going on to the second item. The trainer may begin talking about the first item to help set the pace and tone, trying to keep his or her comments to less than five minutes.

> • Tell the group something about your experience of divorce, perhaps focusing on one thing particularly painful for you, and one thing positive that has resulted.
> • Why did you decide to help with this seminar?

Encourage interaction and occasional questioning among members of the group. At the end, reflect briefly on the process. Use questions such as "What did you observe happening here? Were people listening? Is the group too large? What did you learn from this experience?"

8:45   Break for five minutes.

8:50   Resume the sharing, as above, until it is completed. Then go on to the following.

Task Orientation Instruction. Distribute copies of "The Role of Enablers" statement and copies of appendix B, "Seminar Topics." Review these in detail. Answer questions and emphasize the importance of the next training sessions.

9:30   *Closing.* Take care of housekeeping details not already attended to in seminar preparation, such as volunteers to run the registration table, refreshments, book sales, setting up chairs, and posting directional signs as needed. Someone should locate a suitable restaurant for post-session socializing.

Announce that next week's training will focus on active listening skills and small-group leadership. Express your appreciation for the trainees' willingness to serve as enablers. Dismiss with prayer.

THE ROLE OF ENABLERS

Enablers are volunteers who have experienced separation or divorce and have been trained in listening skills and group leadership. They serve as small-group leaders, fulfill other seminar leadership and organizational roles, and are also available as a contact to provide listening and support within the limits of their time and ability.

Their main purpose is to enable seminar participants to discover and exercise their own abilities and to take responsibility for themselves. Enablers are not expected to solve problems or give answers to participants. They function more as encouraging role models who take a special interest in other people and assist them in reentry into the single life.

SECOND TRAINING SESSION

OBJECTIVES

1. Developing and improving active listening skills
2. Introducing small-group management skills
3. Practicing participation in a small group

Time Activity

7:30 *Welcome.* Welcome people and ask for comments or questions regarding the seminar and last week's handouts. Clarify as needed.

7:40 *Instruction in Listening Skills.* Hand out "Factors for Good Listening." Survey each point with the group, discuss, and answer questions. Ask each person to comment on his or her own strengths and weaknesses as seen in relation to this function of the enabler. Emphasize that we all have our strong and weak points.

8:00 *Listener Exercise.* Disperse the trainees into groups of three. Each person in turn will assume the roles of speaker, listener. and silent observer. Explain that the goal is to have the listener respond accurately to reflect the speaker's meaning. The speaker begins by telling of a problem he or she is facing. The listener is to respond in one of two ways:

- Repeat, or parrot back, the primary facts;
- Reflect the feeling level, identifying the emotion that may or may not be apparent to the speaker.

This is *not* the time to offer solutions to the speaker's problems. The trainer calls time after allowing five minutes for each interaction, which is to be followed by some assessment from the silent observer on such things as eye contact.

8:20 After each person has played each of the three roles, reconvene the group to discuss how easy or difficult it is to listen and reflect without offering direct solutions. What did the trainees learn about themselves?

Break

8:45 *Instruction.* Hand out "Small-Group Leadership Guidelines." Survey these items with the group and answer any questions concerning them. Emphasize the possible tensions between being an active listener and managing the small-group responsibly.

FACTORS FOR GOOD LISTENING

Energy. Good listeners put a lot of energy into paying attention to the speaker. Quality listening is hard work.

Habits. Exercise regularly, practicing good listening habits wherever you are, to establish the habit of paying attention.

Main ideas. Look for the main idea or feeling, rather than probing for details that may be interesting but irrelevant. Find what is really important to the *speaker,* rather than yourself.

Emotional content. Look for feelings that lie below the surface of words, and reflect these to the speaker. This is a key to the speaker's learning that he is really understood.

Respect. Good listeners show respect for the speaker, even when they do not agree with or understand what is being said.

Voice. Listen for the tone and inflection that give clues to the inner seriousness, level of depth, honesty, or emotion of the speaker.

Withhold judgment. Avoid judging. Let the people be as they are, feeling what they feel. This is the time to accept them gracefully.

Avoid emotional reaction. Know your own areas of sensitivity, associations from past experience, that you would compare emotionally. Avoid judgment or reaction.

Distractions. Listen for the person, avoid thinking of physical features, dress, age, or other secondary details. Fight distractions coming from outside, such as noise. The speaker will appreciate the caring attention.

Time. We can listen faster than we can speak. Use your time to think and listen carefully for the important words. Avoid using time to think of what you would say.

Eye contact. Looking directly at someone keeps you in touch and lets them know you want to understand.

Get off yourself. Avoid thinking of whether you look right or sound smart. Put the speaker at the center of your attention.

Reflect. Repeat what you heard, in summary, and interpret the emotions: "I heard you say . . ." or "It sounds as if you are feeling . . ."

Check yourself. Ask if your comments are correct. Then you will know if you have really understood, and they will want to tell you more.

SMALL-GROUP LEADERSHIP GUIDELINES

1. You are the gatekeeper. It is your responsibility to start the group on time. It is also up to you to take the initiative to wrap up the discussion at the end of the allotted time.

2. You must set the pace of sharing by sharing from your own experience in an open and vulnerable way. But don't rattle on. Do your sharing in five minutes or less.

3. Turn to a hesitant speaker and say, "Is there anything you want to add?" Help control dominant talkers.

4. Be permissive. Learn to accept what people share without being judgmental. Say, "Thank you for sharing that, I know it must have been hard." Don't express astonishment at what people share. Give people permission to be who they are and where they

are. People will gradually open up. This may be the first time anyone listened to them. For some, especially men, it may be the first time they make themselves vulnerable.

5. Keep things in balance. Be instrumental in giving everyone who wants to speak an opportunity to do so. Don't be afraid to relinquish control of the group as things progress. Listen and reflect. Don't use up group time to do your own sharing.

6. Enablers must accept the principle of not dating people in the seminar. Those who attend are seeking help and are vulnerable to others because of their emotional unrest.

7. If you feel someone's needs are greater than the group can handle adequately, tell the seminar chairman. He may choose to refer the person to a professional counselor.

8. If you feel inadequate, ask for encouragement. It may cause you some stress to be sharing from your painful past. Talk to the chairman if you are having difficulty in any particular aspect that affects your leadership performance.

9:10   *Practice Group.* Divide into groups of six to nine people. Appoint one enabler leader and one assistant for each group. Instruct them to facilitate the group as if they had just heard the first seminar lecture. Distribute "Discussion Sheet 1" (see ch. 9) and announce that they will have twenty-five minutes to help the group get acquainted and share responses to the discussion sheet. (Enablers who have had previous experience should use discussion sheets 3 or 6 instead.)

Alternative Exercise. The following exercise will help the trainees experience the kind of values conflict they can expect to encounter in this kind of seminar. Divide the trainees into groups of six or more, and distribute a copy of the exercise "The Desert." The groups should discuss their responses and then, if any time remains, consider how the small-group guidelines have been applied.

The Desert

Ten people are stranded in a desert, and your rescue helicopter can save only five. The other five must be left to perish. The people are:

An army captain   Miss America
A twelve-year-old boy   A wealthy society matron
A medical doctor   A college president
A college football player   A bricklayer
A noted preacher   A noted scientist

Which five should be saved, and why?

9:35   Call the total body together to debrief and share comments on how their groups functioned. What did they learn from the process?

9:45   *Close.* Attend to any necessary announcements or arrangements. Firm up details from last week.

Announce that the trainees' homework for the week is to practice listening and reflecting skills during some of their normal encounters and to report back at the next session. Dismiss with prayer.

THIRD TRAINING SESSION

OBJECTIVES
1. Enhancing awareness of personal strengths and weaknesses regarding the task of enabler
2. Further enhancing listening skills and small-group management
3. Enabler pairs becoming acquainted and making plans for how they will share responsibilities

Time Activity

7:30   *Welcome.* Ask some of the group to share experiences from the past week, during which they were to use their listening skills.

7:45   *Group Exercise.* Divide into groups of six to nine people. Give one person in each group a ball of yarn. Instruct the groups that the ball of yarn must be passed to anyone who speaks; the person passing the ball holds onto the end of the string. Even when someone interrupts or initiates a comment, the yarn ball must be passed to that person. Begin by having the person with the yarn ball ask a question of someone else in the group.

Reflection on the Process. After about fifteen to twenty minutes, call the activity to a halt. Point out that during the talking, a pattern emerges with multiple lines of yarn vividly illustrating the amount of involvement and interaction of individuals and the dynamics of the group. Let the groups remain to reflect on the patterns that emerged there. Ask for comments on what happened and what they learned.

8:15   *Enabler Teams.* Assign the pairing of enablers to work together in the forthcoming seminar. Ask them to meet in pairs and discuss the following:

- Their hopes and fears regarding the seminar
- Their particular strengths and weaknesses for the task
- How they will share the responsibilities: who will lead the group the first week, and how they will share leadership thereafter

8:35   Break

8:40   *Problem Solving.* Discuss the handout "Problems Enablers Face" with the whole body. Ask the trainees to respond how they would handle the kinds of situations presented. Let them generate most of the solutions, and add your own only if they are not successful after sufficient time is allowed.

At the end, close the discussion by once again encouraging enablers to recognize their personal tendencies, strengths, and weaknesses. Emphasize that they should apply extra effort to counteract their tendencies. For example, if they like to take charge and give advice, or if they prefer to be passive, they need to apply themselves to the opposite skill.

9:15   *Overview of Miscellaneous Duties.* Hand out a list of weekly responsibilities that enablers must attend to in their groups— seeing to it that participants fill out surveys, for example. Review to clarify as needed. Distribute the enabler list with telephone numbers and instructions that if an emergency prevents any from attending a session, they must notify their partners and then the chairman. Distribute the "Enabler Commitment" statements for signing.

9:30   *Closing.* Answer any remaining questions. Emphasize the value of the adventure ahead. Dismiss with prayer.

Evaluation

1. Hold brief meetings for enablers after the second session and perhaps again later. A more extensive support-evaluation time might be welcomed, so consider a separate evening for that instead of a short one during the second session.

2. Plan a dinner and evaluation meeting for enablers within two weeks after the seminar ends. Consider providing funds for the dinner in the original seminar budget. Conduct a general evaluation of the total seminar at that time. Collect names of participants who are good prospects for serving as enablers in future seminars.

3. Keep the group assignment sheets that were used in the seminar so that when people volunteer later to serve as enablers, you can ask their former enablers for an opinion if any of the volunteers are unknown to you.

PROBLEMS ENABLERS FACE

1. *Quiet People:* Let people remain quiet at first. Approach them outside the group: "I see you didn't have much to say. I hope you're getting something out of the seminar." When discussion in the group dies down, establish eye contact with a quiet person. This will encourage him or her to talk. Don't pressure people to speak; instead, give encouragement.

2. *Dominant People:* Let dominant people speak their piece. If they pause momentarily, say, "Thank you. I wonder if someone else has something they'd like to add." Look at others immediately when asking the next question. If after two weeks the same people are still dominating, approach them at coffee time. Say, "Thanks for helping the group to get off to a good start. Sharing comes easy for you, but it is not so easy for others. Perhaps you could pause for a moment to let some of the quieter people respond too."

3. *People Overwhelmed With Emotion:* Reach out and touch the hand of a person who is having difficulty controlling emotions. Say, "I appreciate how painful this is." If the person leaves the group, let the assistant enabler join him or her, if that seems appropriate.

4. *People With All the Answers:* If someone thinks he or she has all the answers, approach the person outside the group and say, "If you give people all the answers, they won't find the answers within themselves."

ENABLER COMMITMENT

I am willing to assume the responsibility of being an enabler.

I will work to serve the participants in the Coping with Divorce Seminar, and—with sensitivity, caring, and confidentiality—I will pay particular attention to the needs of the people in my group. I want to be part of a team, and, therefore, I will be happy to support and uphold my fellow enablers and to offer my encouragement to assist them in their efforts.

Date: _____

Signed: _____

ENABLER CONVERSATION SUGGESTIONS

FOR THE GROUP'S FIRST TIME TOGETHER:

"Hello! My name is _____. I have volunteered to help lead a group for this seminar. My role is simply to help the group move along in a way that will help us all to get the most out of the seminar. If you have any questions or concerns now or later about how the seminar works, just ask me or one of the other leaders. There are usually two enablers in each group. To get started, if you will look at your discussion sheet, you will see there is a get-acquainted question. Who would like to introduce himself first?"

8

HOW TO GET STARTED

PERSONNEL

Organizing Committee. The organizing committee comprises a chairman, enablers, and other volunteers interested in helping to present the seminar.

Team of Enablers. For a seminar with 49 registrants, there should be a team of 15 enablers, which allows one spare. This allows seven groups of seven members, with two enablers for each group. It is best to have an equal number of men and women as enablers.

Host for Seminar. The host serves as the emcee and should be a person who is hospitable and helps people feel comfortable. He provides continuity throughout the seminar and sees that delegated responsibilities are all carried out, such as the groups' placement, registration, refreshments, and announcements.

Speakers. Speakers can be recruited from among professionals in service fields, such as teachers, or from among talented divorced persons. It is best if the speaker can share personal experiences of crises.

Workers-Helpers. People need to be assigned to receive registrations and fees, prepare materials (brochures, discussion sheets, bibliography, etc.), handle registrations at the door, distribute name tags, pay

We have included here all the basic material needed to conduct a successful seminar. However, a manual with these and other helpful materials, available in handy loose-leaf form and ready for photocopying, may be ordered for ten dollars directly from the Good News Community. Ask for the "Coping With Divorce Manual" from the Good News Community, 4319 Byron Center Avenue S.W., Grand Rapids, MI 49509.

bills, provide books, manage the physical facilities, and serve refreshments.

TRAINING ENABLERS

The training program for enablers is dealt with in chapter 7. Two sessions of three hours each are sufficient to provide proper training.

MATERIALS AND RESOURCES

Discussion sheets, singles' resources in the community, bibliography, copies of the book selected as the main resource,* and other handouts included in chapter 9.

LOCATION

Choose a location on neutral ground. If one purpose of the seminar is to reach the unchurched, avoid holding the seminar in a church building. Instead chose a community building, library, school or similar facility that has a large meeting room and adjacent smaller rooms for small-group activities.

TIMING

Both the initial community contacts and the selection of a meeting place should be made three to six months before the seminar is to be held.

PUBLICITY

Brochures, news releases to the media, cover letters to churches, social service agencies, counselors, attorneys who specialize in divorce, and media advertising should all be considered as potential means for publicity (see appendix A).

MONEY

A seminar will require $500 to $1,000 seed money. This can be remitted through registrations. We recommend having a registration fee of $35. Seek to enlist churches to underwrite a partial amount of the costs (perhaps $250), and solicit businesses with a public relations budget to contribute product or funds.

---

*We recommend Jim Smoke's *Growing Through Divorce* (Irving, Calif.: Harvest House, 1976).

SEMINAR PREPARATION AND DIRECTION CHECKLIST

Seminar Date: _____   *Location:* _____

Category	Advance Time	Date Needed	By Whom
Set dates and secure site	3 months	_____	_____
Order seminar books	3 months	_____	_____
Select manager/assistant manager; organize meeting details; select enablers	2 months	_____	_____
Publicity begins (see "Publicity Checklist")	2 months	_____	_____
Printing brochures begins	3 months	_____	_____
Select enablers (manager/assistant/director)	2 months	_____	_____
Notify enablers of training site	7 weeks	_____	_____
Plan training of enablers/review training materials/revise if necessary	7 weeks	_____	_____
Print all training materials	5 weeks	_____	_____
Secure assistants to handle operation of the following starred items:	8 weeks	_____	_____
Receive registrations/fees, send acknowledgments, prepare name tags/assign participants to groups	6 weeks	_____	_____
Type directory for the seminar	4 weeks	_____	_____
Review all seminar materials/revise as needed	5 weeks	_____	_____
Print all seminar materials	4 weeks	_____	_____
Secure assistant to handle refreshments	4 weeks	_____	_____
Confirm all speakers in writing, include topic summary to total seminar	one month in advance	_____	_____

1 _____   2 _____   3 _____
4 _____   5 _____   6 _____
7 _____   8 _____

Category	Advance Time	Date Needed	By Whom
Call speaker to remind him of the date	48 hours	_____	_____
Registration table attendants to distribute materials, collect unpaid fees, sell books	each week	_____	_____
Supervise facilities	each week	_____	_____
Set up PA system, chairs, tables, as needed	each week	_____	_____

PUBLICITY CHECKLIST

Category	Advance Time	Date Needed	By Whom
Design and print brochure	3 months	_____	_____
Letter/phone contacts with radio/TV/newspaper media: Interviews about 2–3 weeks before seminar	10 weeks	_____	_____
Develop alternative publicity contacts: personnel departments, bar association, libraries	9 weeks	_____	_____
Write/revise special letters to professional mailing lists	8 weeks	_____	_____
Write/revise news release	8 weeks	_____	_____
Print letters and envelopes	8 weeks	_____	_____
Schedule newspaper advertising to begin 4 weeks prior	7 weeks	_____	_____
Get special addressing done (attorneys/counselors lists/churches) and mail to all the above	6 weeks	_____	_____
Send news releases (religion editor, community news, etc.)	6 weeks	_____	_____
Send or deliver brochures to libraries/employers/grocery stores	5 weeks	_____	_____
Post brochures at apartments/laundromats/community buildings	4 weeks	_____	_____

CO-CHAIRPERSON RESPONSIBILITIES
BEFORE SEMINAR BEGINS

1. A meeting will be arranged by the trainer approximately 8 weeks in advance to—
   a. Select 15 to 18 enablers.
   b. Review training materials and learn the responsibilities of those participating.
   c. Learn the roles of the co-chairs in running the seminar sessions, introducing speakers, announcements, etc.

2. The co-chairs have a list of enablers. They are responsible for securing alternates.

3. Secure or confirm location of training.

4. Arrange for refreshments at training sessions.

5. Select persons for seminar to—
   a. Manage the registration table.
   b. Manage the refreshments.

6. At the training sessions, the trainer will be responsible for taking charge, presenting information, and managing training experiences. He will introduce the co-chairpersons who will preside at appropriate times. Special details to be taken care of at those times will be finding enablers who will be willing to—
   a. Post signs at the location of the seminar the first two nights.
   b. Act as floor manager (when furniture needs to be arranged or rearranged or clean-up is necessary).
   c. Arrange for meeting place for social time following seminar nights.
   d. Head social committee that will be making plans for seminar closing party.

9

DISCUSSION SHEETS
AND SEMINAR HANDOUTS

This chapter contains various forms that will be useful in conducting the Coping With Divorce Seminar. These forms may be photocopied without written or oral permission and distributed to the seminar participants. The forms are as follows:

- Identifying Feelings/Emotions
- Goals
- Enabler Evaluation
- Interest Survey
- Seminar Evaluation
- Resources for Singles
- A discussion sheet for each session

IDENTIFYING FEELINGS/EMOTIONS

Feelings are real. Our emotions literally affect our bodies—our heartbeat slows or quickens, we breathe rapidly or slowly, deeply or shallowly. It's natural that our feelings, our emotional state, will be affected by divorce.

Sometimes even when we relate painful experiences we talk about what we think and not about our feelings. In this seminar we want to talk about our feelings, our emotions.

Why? Because while emotions and feelings are real, they also can change. If our emotions are going to change in a positive direction, we need to get in touch with our feelings and be able to identify and express them. Learning to talk about feelings is often a key to resolving our problems and going on to a healthier, happier life.

How do we know when we're in touch with feelings? We use feeling words to describe our inner experiences. Here are some feeling words that may be useful during the seminar. Look them over, and take an extra five minutes or so to brainstorm with your group for other feeling words that describe your divorce experience.

Examples of Emotions

joy	jealousy	boredom	caution
sorrow	hope	uneasiness	relief
love	sadness	elation	uselessness
hate	embarrassment	uncertainty	pride
pain	loneliness	weariness	happiness
grief	calm	anxiety	fear
rejection	confidence	silliness	anger
gladness	discomfort	contentment	hopefulness

GOALS

This practice sheet is designed to help you set goals for yourself and work toward those goals.

Goals may be short-term (one week, one month), or long-term (six months, six years). Goals may relate to any aspect of life: career, education, finances, spiritual, social, or any other.

Objectives are steps, events, decisions, or actions that are part of our progression along the way to our goals. These should be as specific and concrete as possible so that we can tell if they have been achieved and measurable progress made.

Time is important. It is always helpful to set dates for both goals and objectives.

Goal   **Target Dates**

_____   _____

Objectives: (Be specific. Name things, places, decisions, persons, if their help is needed.)

_____   _____

_____   _____

_____   _____

_____   _____

Goal   **Target Dates**

_____   _____

Objectives:

_____   _____

_____   _____

_____   _____

_____   _____

ENABLER EVALUATION

Group No. _____

Enabler: Male _____ Female _____

Participants, we would appreciate your honest appraisal of the function of the enablers in your group. There are several specific ways that they are supposed to be contributing to the success of your group experience. Please rate this person by checking your choice in the following categories:

	Too Little	Adequate	Good	Too Much
1. Takes charge, keeps control of group activity.	_____	_____	_____	_____
2. Shows a caring attitude toward participants.	_____	_____	_____	_____
3. Listens well to the participants.	_____	_____	_____	_____
4. Provides stimulating comments or experiences of his/her own.	_____	_____	_____	_____
5. Helps participants understand the ideas presented in the seminar.	_____	_____	_____	_____

INTEREST SURVEY

Here are some ways to get involved in our seminar program:

SEMINARS

_____ Enabler
_____ Registration table
_____ Planning seminars/committee work
_____ Refreshments
_____ Publicity

OFFICE TASKS

(Mailing, Telephone, Communications)

You don't need secretarial skills.

_____ Office volunteer   Morning _____

                                 Afternoon _____

NEWSLETTER

_____ Typing
_____ Layout
_____ Selling ads
_____ Art work

SPECIAL SKILLS

_____

_____

Name _____

Home Telephone _____ Work Telephone _____

(List work phone only if you may receive calls at your job.)

SEMINAR EVALUATION

Please be frank in your criticism. We need your comments, both negative and positive, to improve the seminar.

1. What has the seminar meant to you? _____
_____
_____
_____

2. Rate the sessions. Place a check in the spaces to indicate the two most helpful and the two least helpful sessions.

	Most Helpful	Least Helpful
a. Facing Reality	____	____
b. Letting Go of the Past	____	____
c. What Really Happened?	____	____
d. Taking Responsibility for Yourself	____	____
e. Reaching Out From Loneliness	____	____
f. Growing Through Your Divorce	____	____
g. Friendship and Dating	____	____
h. Living the Single Life	____	____

3. Are there topics that need more or better treatment? Do you have any comments on the general approach and format of the meetings? _____
_____
_____
_____
_____

4. Would you recommend the seminar to a friend? _____

5. Please give the names of one or two participants in your group whom you feel have the most potential for serving as enablers. ____
_____

OPTIONAL: Name _____

Home Telephone _____ Work Telephone _____

RESOURCES FOR SINGLES

SUPPORT GROUPS

Name _____   Phone No. _____

Address _____

Name _____   Phone No. _____

Address _____

HOUSING

Salvation Army(?)   Phone No. _____

Address _____

Local Domestic Crisis Center   Phone No. _____

Address _____

NATIONAL ORGANIZATIONS, RESOURCES

The National Association of Christian Singles
P.O. Box 11394
Kansas City, MO 64112

Spirit Magazine (formerly *Solo*)
P.O. Box 1231
Sisters, OR 97759

Christian Single
Sunday School Board
127 Ninth Ave. North
Nashville, TN 37234

EMERGENCY

Local Domestic Crisis Center   Phone No. _____

Address _____

Local Information and Referral Center   Phone No. _____

Address _____

Police Department   Phone No. _____

Address _____

Rape Crisis Center   Phone No. _____

Address _____

MONETARY

Credit Counseling Center   Phone No. _____
Address _____

Housing Assistance Center   Phone No. _____
Address _____

Family Budget Service   Phone No. _____
Address _____

Food Stamps/Dept. of Social Services   Phone No. _____

Emergency Funding   Phone No. _____
Address _____

SUBSTANCE ABUSE

Alcoholics Anonymous   Phone No. _____
Address _____

Local Drug Rehabilitation Center   Phone No. _____
Address _____

CHILDREN

Center for and about Teens   Phone No. _____
Address _____

County Food Supplement Program   Phone No. _____
Address _____

Parents Anonymous   Phone No. _____
Address _____

SENIOR CITIZENS

American Assn. of Retired People   Phone No. _____
Address _____

Area Agency on Aging   Phone No. _____
Address _____

LEGAL

NAACP   Phone No. _____
Address _____

Bar Association   Phone No. _____
Address _____

Better Business Bureau   Phone No. _____
Address _____

Civil Liberties Union   Phone No. _____
Address _____

Civil Rights   Phone No. _____
Address _____

Legal Aid   Phone No. _____
Address _____

Friend of the Court   Phone No. _____
Address _____

Welfare Rights   Phone No. _____
Address _____

COUNSELING SERVICES

Name _____   Phone No. _____
Address _____

Women's Resource Center   Phone No. _____
Address _____

Christian Counseling Center   Phone No. _____
Address _____

Teen Counseling Center   Phone No. _____
Address _____

EDUCATION/JOB TRAINING

Local Community Ed. Dept.   Phone No. _____
Address _____

Local Junior College   Phone No. _____
Address _____

A telephone directory and the local library are useful sources for obtaining the information needed to complete this list.

DISCUSSION SHEET
COPING WITH DIVORCE SEMINAR

Session 1: Facing Reality

1. Introductions:

Give your name. Tell something about yourself you would like the others to know.

2. Sharing:

Which of the emotional stages mentioned tonight (and listed below) have you experienced most vividly? Share something about your experience.

SHOCK/DENIAL. Emotional numbness, inability to comprehend what's happening. Refusal to admit the loss of the marriage, denial to friends, even to self.

ANGER/GUILT. Letting out pent-up feelings toward spouse, in-laws, others. Wishing spouse were dead, often followed by a sense of guilt.

DEPRESSION. Feelings of failure, hopelessness, thoughts of suicide, fanticizing about what might have been, sometimes withdrawal from family and friends.

BARGAINING. Hoping for extra time to put off the pain that's coming, or for time to change the situation.

RESIGNATION. Giving in to misery, accepting pity. Or ACCEPTANCE. Accepting the reality, with the hope for something good to come out of the experience.

3. Optional:

If someone helped you move through these stages, share how it happened.

4. Assignment: Begin a personal journal, to record your own journey as we move through the next few sessions. Reflect in writing on what you experience and record your thoughts tonight for the first page of your journal.

5. Growth activity: Call one person in your group this week.

6. Reading assignment: *Growing Through Divorce*, chs. 1, 2, 3.

DISCUSSION SHEET
COPING WITH DIVORCE SEMINAR

Session 2: Letting Go

1. Reentry:

Do you have any comments on your experiences this past week?

2. Rethinking the past:

How have you experienced "letting go" of your married life (e.g., ties to spouse, children, house/home, friends, pets)?

Which has been most difficult or confusing?

(Optional: Do you recall any dreams that seem to relate to letting go of married life?)

3. Evaluating the present:

Describe your current feelings about your spouse/ex-spouse. How would you like to feel about him/her?

Have you experienced intense feelings that are hard to manage or let go of?

4. Envisioning the future:

What are you doing—or what could you do—to gain new experiences, friendships, or an occupation to fill the empty space in your life and build a new identity for yourself?

Choose a specific goal, one thing you can do this week to work toward your personal development goal.

5. Reading assignment:

Growing Through Divorce, ch. 4.

DISCUSSION SHEET
COPING WITH DIVORCE SEMINAR

Session 3: What Really Happened?

1. Reentry: Any comments on your experience this past week?

2. Rethinking the past: What did you learn about relationships tonight that helped you understand the past?

   Is there something you wish you had known when you got married?

   Can you identify clearly one or more aspects of your relationship in which you contributed to its breakdown?

3. Evaluating the present: How do your family or friends affect your ability to accept the past, to leave it behind and learn something from it?

4. Envisioning the future: Is there a specific area in which you would like to learn or grow?

5. Growth activity: Write down in your journal this week at least two reasons that your relationship broke down.

6. Reading assignment: *Growing Through Divorce*, chs. 5, 6.

DISCUSSION SHEET
COPING WITH DIVORCE SEMINAR

Session 4: Taking Responsibility for Yourself

1. Reentry: Any comments on your experience this past week?

2. Past and Present: What are some of your feelings about the past you would like to let go of?

   What are some of the struggles you are having in taking responsibility for your present situation?

3. Envisioning the future.   If you knew you could not fail, what is one thing you would really like to do?

   List three or more things you are looking forward to in the next few weeks (or name at least three things you enjoy doing).

   _____

   _____

   _____

   Consider the goals sheet you have been given and discuss how you will use it.

4. Growth activity: Do one thing this week to be "good to yourself."

5. Reading assignment: *Growing Through Divorce*, ch. 7.

(Copyright © 1984, Good News Community, used by permission.)

DISCUSSION SHEET
COPING WITH DIVORCE SEMINAR

Session 5: Reaching Out From Loneliness

1. Reentry:

Evelute your personal growth through divorce to this particular point.

2. Rethinking the past:

How have your concepts and feelings about "family" been affected by your divorce?

Has your experience in this seminar taught you something about your need for "alternate family" or a social support network?

3. Evaluating the present:

If you have a supportive family around you, describe how you feel about it, and how it helps you. How is your church or religious affiliation proving helpful at this time?

Have you found ways to have good "alone" times without being lonely?

4. Envisioning the future:

What more could you be doing to find new people and new experiences to overcome loneliness, rejection, and bad memories?

5. Goal for this week:

What one thing can I do this week or plan for later to strengthen my own support system or circle of "family" and friends?

6. Reading assignment:

Growing Through Divorce, chs. 8, 11.

(Copyright © 1984, Good News Community, used by permission.)

DISCUSSION SHEET
COPING WITH DIVORCE SEMINAR

Session 6: Growing Through Your Divorce

While the group is getting started tonight, look over the special "Interest Survey." Find a place where you might consider getting involved. Consult the enablers for explanation of any items listed or for other information about the organization. This is one way to get started growing!

1. Rethinking the past: Have you experienced a need for forgiveness in your divorce? With spouse, with God, or others.

   How have other people helped your memories to heal? Has your personal faith given you help with this?

2. Evaluating the present: Do you sometimes feel a need for different kinds of intimacy that are hard to fulfill? Are you satisfied with how you deal with these needs? What would you like to do differently?

3. Envisioning the future: What more do you see needs to take place in your growth?

   What are some of the ways you are learning to overcome lonliness, rejection and bad memories?

4. Growth activity: Write a list at home this week of "Ten things I like about myself." Bring it to the session next week.

5. Reading assignment: *Growing Through Divorce*, chs. 9, 10.

   Think of questions or concerns you have that so far have not been addressed in the seminar. Write them down and bring them to next week's session.

DISCUSSION SHEET
COPING WITH DIVORCE SEMINAR
Session 7: Friendship and Dating

1. Reentry: What is one new step in the rediscovery of being single that you have experienced this week?

2. Evaluating the present: Picture yourself in each of the following situations. Imagine how you would respond at this time and how you might respond differently a few months from now. Take a few minutes to think about it or make notes before going on with the discussion of your answers.

• A person of the opposite sex, whom you've seen or spoken to only briefly before, calls you. He or she says, "I've been wanting to see [name of movie] and I'd like to go this weekend. I thought you might enjoy it too. We could go just as friends, not necessarily a 'date.' What do you think?"

• Someone of the opposite sex calls you and says, "I'm having a few people over Sunday night to play 'Trivial Pursuit.' I'm looking for one more guest so there would be six of us. Would you be interested?" When you ask who else is coming, he or she names two men and two women. How would you respond?

• Someone whom you've met or seen in meetings or groups has caught your attention. At some point this person has given you a "positive signal" of encouragement. You would like to know him or her better. What would you say or do?

• You are on your first or second date with someone. You have had a pleasant time. Now he or she says, "How about stopping at my place for a drink or coffee?" How would you respond? What would you consider in deciding how to respond?

• Your mother, your father, or a family friend calls to ask you over for dinner on a Saturday night. This is the second week in a row you reply that you can't come, since you have plans to go out. They say, "It seems to me that you've been awfully busy lately. Don't you think you are overdoing it, running around so much?" How do you reply?

3. Envisioning the future: What will you do this week to enhance your friendships?

4. Reading assignment: *Growing Through Divorce,* chs. 12, 14, 15.

DISCUSSION SHEET
COPING WITH DIVORCE SEMINAR

Session 8: Living the Single Life

1. Reentry:

Share any experiences you've had this week that illustrate your developing new friends, "family," or circles of support.

2. Evaluating the present:

Do you think it is possible to feel like a whole person even when single?

Which things in your life offer the most challenge in feeling good about yourself as a single person?

3. Envisioning the future:

Can you identify certain things that you need to learn more about in order to handle them as a single person? (For example, dating, taking care of your property, car, family, business, or social invitations.)

Say "Thank you" to someone in this group who has helped you grow as a single person.

Discuss whether your group will meet again occasionally. Make plans now for those who wish to meet or to attend a "Creative Growth" meeting, or some other activity together.

What goal can you identify this week that would help you take better charge of your life as a single?

10

LEADERS NOTES AND SEMINAR MATERIALS

WEEK 1

ANNOUNCEMENTS

1. Welcome the participants.

2. Remind the participants to pick up their name tags and materials each week and to return their name tags when they leave.

3. Ask the participants to be punctual, since the sessions will start on time.

4. Inform participants of smoking restrictions.

5. Tonight's talk is "Facing Reality." Introduce the speaker.

6. After the talk, announce that you will break for coffee. Ask the participants to get their refreshments and go to their assigned groups right away. Give the location of each group.

7. "If for any reason you must request to be put in another group, we will try to arrange that for you."

IMPORTANT GUIDELINES

These guidelines should be declared to all the participants.

1. Remember everyone's right to confidentiality.

2. Give everyone a chance to speak who desires to speak.

3. Be sensitive to the others in your group.

4. Be responsible to help your group be effective.

MATERIALS NEEDED

1. Have a complete check-in list so that you know if anyone hasn't paid.
2. Enablers should have a list of the participants in their group.
3. Discussion sheet 1 should be handed out to the participants as they arrive.
4. Optional: A stress chart is available in the book *Stress/Unstress* by Keith Sehnert, M.D. (Minneapolis: Augsburg, 1981).
5. Name tags with small-group numbers assigned should be handed out as participants arrive.
6. A book for each participant and enabler should be handed out on their arrival.

ENABLER DINNER

Make plans for the enabler dinner, which is to be held within two weeks after the end of the seminar. Remember to announce there will be a brief meeting of all enablers after next week's session. One of speakers from the panel on the last week will want to ask for donations.

WEEK 2

ANNOUNCEMENTS

1. Welcome the participants.

2. "Small-group name/phone number lists will be given to you by your enablers. If you want to be included in the seminar directory, please sign up on a list to be circulated during small-group time."

3. "Enablers will have a brief meeting immediately after this seminar session."

4. "If you missed the first session of the seminar, obtain your copy of the book we are using. Any time you miss a session, you can pick up materials from previous weeks."

5. "A book table will be available each week with books you may be interested in purchasing."

6. The topic tonight is "Letting Go of the Past." Introduce the speaker.

MATERIALS NEEDED

1. Group sheets with names and phone numbers for each group. An empty sheet for each group to sign up to be in the seminar directory.
2. Discussion sheet 2.
3. The bibliography sheet.
4. "Emotions Vocabulary" sheet.
5. The book table is available for the convenience of the participants.
6. Extra copies of the text are available if any participant would like to buy one for a friend.

WEEK 3

ANNOUNCEMENTS

1. Welcome the participants. Remind them about their name tags.

2. "The book table is still available. If you have missed any seminar sessions, be sure to pick up materials from past weeks."

3. "Participants may still sign up to be in the directory if they weren't here last week."

4. "The topic next week is 'Taking Responsibility for Yourself.' Tonight's topic is 'What Really Happened.'" Introduce the speaker.

MATERIALS NEEDED

1. Seminar directory sign-up sheet
2. Discussion sheet 3
3. "Resources for Singles" sheet
4. Books for sale

WEEK 4

ANNOUNCEMENTS

1. Welcome the participants. Remind them about their name tags.

2. "The book table is still available. If you have missed any seminar sessions, be sure to pick up materials from past weeks."

3. "Participants may still sign up to be in the directory if they weren't here last week."

4. "The topic next week will be 'Reaching Out From Loneliness.' Tonight's topic is 'Taking Responsibility for Yourself.'" Introduce the speaker.

Announcement after the talk: "As one form of taking responsibility for yourself, we want you to give an evaluation of your enabler's work to this point. Please fill out the form and turn it in to the evaluation sheet box at the registration desk tonight."

MATERIALS NEEDED

1. Discussion sheet 4
2. Goal sheet
3. Directory of seminar participants
4. Enabler evaluation forms

Chairman: Collect the "Enabler Evaluation" forms after the meeting. During the week, bundle them together for each enabler. Look them over with your co-chairman if this is possible. Make notes if there are any problems you need to discuss with any enablers.

WEEK 5

ANNOUNCEMENTS

1. "If you did not get your directory last week, pick up one this week."

2. The topic next week is "Growing Through Your Divorce." The topic this week is "Reaching Out From Loneliness." Introduce the speaker.

3. After the speaker's address, announce: "We are going to form a temporary social committee to plan an event for the end of the seminar. We need one or two participants from each group. Two enablers have already volunteered to work with you.

MATERIALS NEEDED

1. Discussion sheet 5
2. Directories

WEEK 6

ANNOUNCEMENTS

1. A report from the social committee should be given concerning the get-together at the end of the seminar.

2. "Enablers, please plan to attend an evaluation dinner." Give the enablers the date.

3. "Next week the topic will be 'Friendship and Dating.' The topic tonight is 'Growing Through Divorce.'" Introduce the speaker.

MATERIALS NEEDED

1. Discussion sheet 6

WEEK 7

ANNOUNCEMENTS

1. Distribute the "Interest Survey" sheets. "Please use this sheet to indicate where you may be able to contribute to future seminars."

2. "Next week we will have a panel of four people to discuss living the single life. The topic tonight is 'Friendship and Dating.'" Introduce the speaker.

MATERIALS NEEDED

1. Discussion sheet 7
2. "Interest Survey" sheets
3. Letters inviting enablers to their appreciation dinner. Distribute these to the enablers.

WEEK 8

SCHEDULE

7:30–7:35 Welcome and announcements
7:35–8:20 Panel of speakers
8:20–8:30 Break
8:30–9:20 Discussion time
9:20–9:30 Fill out seminar evaluation sheets

ANNOUNCEMENTS

1. Announcements from the social committee.

2. Announce schedule for the evening.

3. When you introduce the panel of speakers, encourage them to limit their comments to about five minutes each to allow time for questions from the participants. As you introduce them, announce the topic on which they will be speaking.

MATERIALS NEEDED

1. Discussion sheet 8
2. Optional: Posters
3. Seminar evaluation sheets

Announcement: "We hope this seminar has been helpful to you . . ." with suitable closing comments and thanks to all the volunteers.

APPENDIX A

PUBLICIZING THE SEMINAR

When it's time to have seminar brochures printed (see chapter 8), choose paper of good quality. This will promote respect for your organization by creating a favorable image. If possible, use colored printing ink also. The letterhead should also be high-quality paper; this will create a good image throughout the community and promote good public relations, advertising, and marketing.

While brochures and cover letters are being printed, compile a mailing list. Be sure to include churches, pastors, personnel directors, educators, and legal offices with family practices. The library may be helpful in locating these sources; the local Chamber of Commerce should have address labels for local businesses. A list of attorneys can be obtained from the American Bar Association, and phone calls locally will indicate which law firms specialize in family practice. Approximately 20 percent of law offices handle divorce cases.

Advertise in the newspaper. There are free community events columns that should be used. For the first seminar you might request that the community events editor write a feature about it. This provides excellent free publicity. You should anticipate spending about half of the seminar budget on advertising, at least until your organization has established some recognition in the community.

Place ads in the entertainment section, not only in the religion section. Since men are more reluctant than women to sign up for the seminar, it is also a good idea to run ads in the business and sports sections.

Flyers are another effective means of publicity. They can be placed in apartment offices, grocery stores, laundromats, and other buildings where the public is served.

Compile a list of publicity release outlets. Contact a hospital or another local institution that would already have such lists. They are usually willing to share this information. The list would include radio and television stations, cable TV stations, the city magazine, newspapers, and local talk-show hosts.

Chapter 8 gives information on how far in advance each step should be taken.

APPENDIX B

SEMINAR TOPICS

The purpose of this appendix is to provide you and your speakers with a few ideas central to each of the session topics. This information is useful at the time a speaker is enlisted for the seminar, because it helps the planners and speaker alike to have common expectations as to central theme and significant ideas that should be covered.

FIRST WEEK

In the first week of the seminar it is important to touch the people emotionally. The topic "Facing Reality" takes them through the stages of grieving (see chapter 3). The participants can be helped to understand that the emotional turmoil they are experiencing is normal. Once they have faced the reality that life feels like a jumbled-up jigsaw puzzle, they can begin to put the pieces together again. It's very helpful when the speaker can share from his or her own experience and vulnerability and thus encourage the others to share openly as well.

SECOND WEEK

The topic for the second week is "Letting Go." It is important to put the past away. While the feelings of pain and rejection should not be denied, neither should they hang on as our foremost thoughts. The speaker for this topic should point out the more subtle ways we may avoid letting go, such as spying on the former spouse or taking responsiblilty for his or her well-being. Even continual arguing or a determination to "get even" are negative but significant forms of "holding on." Participants must recognize that they cannot really move healthily into the future until they have sufficiently let go of the past.

THIRD WEEK

The third topic is "What Really Happened?" The speaker must be especially sensitive here, because many participants will feel like victims. It will be painful for them to accept their share of responsibility in the breakdown of their marriages. In his book *Unconditional Love*, John Powell gives three characteristics of unconditional love: kindness, encouragement, and challenge. From these, perhaps the participants could reflect on the following questions to help them understand their culpability in their failed marriages:

- Did I treat my mate as if I was on his or her side?

- Did I support and encourage my mate?

- Did I criticize my mate constructively or destructively?

The speaker's vulnerability and the openness of the enablers will accomplish much in helping people to face up to their past.

FOURTH WEEK

The topic for week 4 is "Taking Responsibility for Yourself." This is the time to emphasize that each person's future depends on his or her own choices. It is time to stop blaming others and realize that one alone must make decisions about work and social life. Overdependence on others is a handicap to freedom. At the same time, healthy interdependency, family ties, and a network of good friends are to be encouraged. The speaker can share how he or she assumed new responsibilities such as getting the car serviced, learning to cook, and making financial decisions. Each achievement gives satisfaction. After some time, feelings of inadequacy grow into feelings of confidence. People grow into the job of coping with their new lives.

FIFTH WEEK

The topic for the fifth week is "Reaching Out From Loneliness." Taking initiative to build new community to replace the loss you have incurred through divorce is very important. Divorce seriously disturbs much of a person's community network, and we often feel as if we have a big hole in our personal fabric of life.

Community can come from family or from people with whom we have emotional, spiritual, or intellectual values in common. Don't let yourself stay shut off, but reach out in these areas. It is also important to have a church that provides personal support and spiritual nourishment and is sensitive to the real needs of a divorced person. People need to realize that they are responsible for their own future through conscious choices of friends, clubs, church, and all the rest of their personal world. They can be encouraged to hold on to those people and relationships that have proved to be loyal through this crisis, while letting go of relationships that are unalterably changed by the divorce.

SIXTH WEEK

"Growing Through Your Divorce" is the sixth topic. This is the time to recognize the good things that are beginning to come out of a divorce. It is helpful to recognize that pain is one way God forces us to examine our ways. Participants are encouraged to look at their values and to reevaluate what really matters in life. These refined values are the fruit of a painful process that God allows, as indicated in Romans 5:3–5 and 8:28.

Accepting forgiveness for oneself and offering to forgive one's former spouse are key emotional doorways to the future. They put an end to guilt and bitterness. A positive working relationship with the former spouse is crucial if the couple had children. Parents can stop acting on the basis of emotions and make rational choices that are good for their children. People usually find also that new challenges and social opportunities help them to grow socially and intellectually.

SEVENTH WEEK

"Friendship and Dating" is the topic for week 7. The speaker needs to illustrate the common fears and anxieties that come with dating at a mature age. People are more vulnerable because of their emotional scars. The twelve types of intimacy identified by researchers Howard and Charlotte Clinebell, as well as other items from the book, *Game Free* by Thomas Odon can help people avoid unhealthy patterns in relationships.

Friendships with both men and women on a nonromantic level is an exciting new option for many people. Friendship can grow into romance, but a fast-paced romance seldom develops into a deep friendship. Most people find that what they really want are some good friends, and in a subsequent marriage they want a true companion.

EIGHTH WEEK

For the eighth week it is good to have a panel of four or five people to talk about how they are handling "the Single Life." This is an excellent opportunity for witnessing and evangelizing as the panelists share how their faith helped them through a difficult aspect of adjustment. Topics that are especially good for the panel to deal with are Handling My Emotions, Dating Again, Handling My Feelings About Sexuality, How I Grew Through My Divorce, and Single Parenting or Weekend Parenting.

Allow a segment of time for the participants to ask questions of the panelists. The participants can be asked to turn in requested topics during the prior week. It is best if the panel is made up of enablers from the seminar, since they already have rapport with some of the audience. People active in the singles ministry in other ways are naturally good possibilities for this role as well. This will encourage people to become involved in other activities when the seminar concludes.

ANNOTATED BIBLIOGRAPHY

There are far more books on divorce than we can know firsthand. The following selection, however, represents the books we have seen that appear to be the most helpful. They are arranged under seven headings.

I. DIVORCE MINISTRY RESOURCES

Reed, Bobbie. *Developing a Single Adult Ministry.* Glendale, Calif.: Regal/GL, 1977.

> Although aimed at the total single-adult population, a handbook that is right on target with practical guidelines for ministry to the divorced.

Smoke, Jim. *Growing Through Divorce.* Eugene, Ore.: Harvest House, 1976.

> One of the most practical, "what-to-do" books for the divorced, with a clear Christian perspective.

Thompson, David A. *Recovering From Divorce.* Minneapolis: Bethany House, 1982.

> In a workbook-style format, a resource useful as the basis for a small discussion group of newly divorced people. Most helpful when supplemented by additional reading material.

II. UNDERSTANDING DIVORCE

Conway, Jim. *Men in Midlife Crisis.* Elgin, Ill.: David C. Cook, 1978.

Conway, Jim, and Sally Conway. *Women in Midlife Crisis.* Wheaton, Ill.: Tyndale, 1983.

> Christian perspectives on one of the most vexing problems involved in causes of divorce.

Correu, Larry M. *Beyond the Broken Marriage.* Philadelphia: Westminster, 1982.

> A well-written overview of the process and challenges facing the newly single person.

Fisher, Bruce. *Rebuilding When Your Relationship Ends.* San Luis Obispo, Calif.: Impact, 1981.

By the developer of "Rebuilding Seminars," used and adapted by hundreds of groups nationwide.

Greteman, James, and Leon Haverkamp. *Divorce and Beyond* Chicago: Buckley, 1983, 1984.

Available in both a participants book and a full Facilitators Manual. Very useful combination, especially suited to Roman Catholics but also useful to Protestants. Deals well with emotional needs.

Hershey, Terry. *Beginning Again*. Laguna Hills, Calif.: Merit, 1984.

See "Selected Program Sources" for program manual and materials by Hershey.

Hosier, Helen Kooiman. *The Other Side of Divorce*. New York: Hawthorn, 1975.

A thoughtful and sensitive examination of the issues from a Christian viewpoint.

Smith, Harold Ivan. *Help for Parents of a Divorced Son or Daughter*. St. Louis: Concordia, 1981.

Uniquely valuable, directed toward the hurting parent.

Smoke, Jim. *Suddenly Single*. Old Tappan, N.J.: Revell, 1982.

Fresh insights from a wise and experienced author.

Trafford, Abigail. *Crazy Time, Surviving Divorce*. New York: Harper & Row, 1982.

One of the best, personable testimonies, well researched, from the secular press.

Weiss, Robert. *Marital Separation*. New York: Basic Books, 1975.

A landmark professional publication, very readable, still among the best available on the subject.

III. CHILDREN AND DIVORCE/SINGLE PARENTING

Barr, Debbie. *Caught in the Crossfire: Children of Divorce*. Grand Rapids: Zondervan, 1986.

A comprehensive report on research that describes the effects of divorce on children and how to deal with them, from a Christian perspective.

Blume, Judy. *It's Not the End of the World*. New York: Dell, 1982.

Helpful and written in the lively style that has made this author's fiction popular among children.

Bustanoby, André. *Being a Single Parent*. Grand Rapids: Zondervan, 1985.

A book covering a wide range of subjects from age-group problems to dating, by a Christian counselor.

Coleman, William. *What Children Need to Know When Parents Get Divorced.* Minneapolis: Bethany House, 1983.

A very helpful Christian resource for parents of children through preteens.

Grollman, Earl. *Talking About Divorce.* Boston: Beacon, 1975.

Drawings and simple language children can understand, plus helpful answers for a child's questions.

Ricci, Isolina. *Mom's House, Dad's House.* New York: Colier, 1982.

How parents can make two homes in positive ways for their children.

Swihart, Judson J., and Steven L. Brigham. *Helping Children of Divorce.* Downers Grove, Ill.: InterVarsity, 1982.

Practical and well-written, includes adolescent issues.

Tickfer, Mildred. *Healing the Hurt.* Grand Rapids: Baker, 1984.

Help for teenagers with divorced parents, from a Christian mental health professional with years of experience working with teens.

Vigeveno, H. S., and Anne Claire. *Divorce and the Children.* Glendale, Calif.: Regal/GL, 1979.

Includes sections relating to living in a stepfamily.

Weiss, Robert. *Going It Alone.* New York: Basic Books, 1979.

Authoritative, broad treatment of single parenting.

IV. PERSONAL AND SPIRITUAL GROWTH FOR SINGLES

Augsburger, David. *Caring Enough to Confront.* Ventura, Calif.: Regal/GL, 1980.

How to understand and express your deepest feelings.

Berry, Karen. *Beyond Broken Dreams.* Cincinnati: St. Anthony Messenger, 1984.

A scriptural pathway to new life.

McAllaster, Elva. *Free to Be Single.* Chappaqua, N.Y.: Christian Herald, 1980.

A wise and personal study of issues that confront every single adult.

O'Collins, Gerald. *The Second Journey.* New York: Paulist Press, 1978.

Spiritual awareness and the midlife crisis.

Powell, John. *Unconditional Love.* Niles, Ill.: Argus, 1978.

An outstanding examination of personal love and the meaning of the gospel.

_____. *Why Am I Afraid to Tell You Who I Am?* Niles, Ill.: Argus, 1969.

A classic examining our fear of vulnerability and what to do about it.

Salter, Debbie. *One Is More Than Un.* Grand Rapids: Baker, 1979.

A handy study for single adults, divorced or never married.

Seamands, David S. *Healing for Damaged Emotions.* Wheaton, Ill.: Victor, 1981.

Scriptural nourishment for delicate needs.

Smedes, Lewis B. *Forgive and Forget.* San Francisco: Harper & Row, 1984.

A thoughtful and practical book to help people get past their hurts and move into the future.

Swindoll, Chuck. *Starting Over.* Portland, Ore.: Multnomah, 1983.

Biblical teachings applied by a popular Christian teacher to the reality of starting anew.

Viscott, David. *Risking.* New York: Pocket Books/Simon & Schuster, 1979.

A potent personal growth book by a common sense pyschiatrist, well-known for other practical books, including *How to Live With Another Person.*

V. SINGLE LIFE, NEW RELATIONSHIPS, DATING

Augsburger, David. *Caring Enough to Hear.* Ventura, Calif.: Regal/GL, 1982.

Practical skills to build and deepen relationships.

Bustanoby, André. *Just Friends?* Grand Rapids: Zondervan, 1986.

What people too often don't know about the meaning of friendship. A Christian guide to making positive relationships, for both single and married adults.

Chavez, Patricia, and Clif Cartland. *Picking Up the Pieces.* Nashville: Thomas Nelson, 1979.

Valuable because of the authors' honesty and vulnerability in relating their experiences in new relationships after divorce.

Johnson, Stephen M. *First Person Singular.* New York: New American Library, 1978.

Soundly based, good advice from a reliable secular professional, relating to many issues of taking charge of one's own life.

McGinnis, Alan Loy. *The Friendship Factor.* Minneapolis: Augsburg, 1979.

Outstanding, practical Christian help for building healthy relationships.

———. *The Romance Factor.* New York: Harper & Row, 1983.

One of the best, most insightful books examining romantic relationships, for both single and married adults.

VI. REMARRIAGE, STEPPARENTING

Brown, Bob W. *Getting Married Again*. Waco, Tex.: Word, 1979.

A Christian guide to successful remarriage.

Bustanoby, André. *The Readymade Family*. Grand Rapids: Zondervan, 1982.

Practical and sound approaches to the challenges of putting two families together and surviving as a stepparent.

Ellisen, Stanley A. *Divorce and Remarriage in the Church*. Rev. ed. Grand Rapids: Zondervan, 1980.

A careful approach to developing a consistent Christian attitude toward remarriage in the church.

Richards, Larry. *Remarriage: Healing Gift From God*. Waco, Tex.: Word, 1981.

An examination of both scriptural and experiential issues.

Roosevelt, Ruth, and Jeannette Lofas. *Living in Step*. New York: McGraw-Hill, 1977.

One of the best books on this issue from the secular press.

VII. CATHOLIC CONCERNS

Carpenter, Sue, et al. *Learning to Live Again*. Cincinnati: St. Anthony Messenger, 1979.

Sometimes used in conjunction with the Beginning Experience weekend retreat, as listed in our "Selected Program Resources." Emphasizes the spiritual journey through grief to a new life.

Maz, Medard. *Helps for the Separated and Divorced*. Liguori, Mo.: Liguori, 1981.

Used by a number of Catholic organizations as the basis for discussion groups.

Young, James J. *Divorcing, Believing, Belonging*. New York: Paulist Press, 1984.

The single best book for Catholics, presenting meditative essays that enable the believer to find a new sense of belonging in the faith.

_____. *Divorce Ministry and the Marriage Tribunal*. New York: Paulist Press, 1982.

Contains chapters by several leaders in the field of ministry to separated and divorced Catholics.

_____. *Ministering to the Divorced Catholic*. New York: Paulist Press, 1979.

VIII. PERIODICALS

The Beginning Experience Team Newsletter. 3100 West 41st Street, Sioux Falls, SD 57105-4292.

See "Selected Program Resources."

Jacob's Well. North American Conference of Separated and Divorced Catholics, 1100 South Goodman Street, Rochester, NY 14620.

National newsletter of this organization.

Journal of Divorce. Haworth Press, 28 East 22nd Street, New York, NY 10010.

Quarterly specializing in clinical studies and research articles from secular sources, and valuable to anyone working in the field. Special rate for institutions.

SALT. Single Adult Institute Training, P.O. Box 1231, Sisters, OR 97759.

Monthly newsletter published by the parent organization, *Solo* magazine.

Single i. Institute of Singles Dynamics, P.O. Box 11394, Kansas City, MO 64112.

Monthly newsletter of events, resources, and groups for leaders of Christian singles, with subscription rate but sent free to all "leadership-level" members of the National Association of Christian Singles. See *Today's Single* below.

Spirit. P.O. Box 1231, Sisters, OR 97759.

Slick, well-produced national magazine for Christian singles. Provides one of the most appealing approaches to the singles scene for a wide audience. Formerly called *Solo.* Six issues per year.

Today's Single. National Association of Christian Singles, 915 West Wisconsin Avenue, Suite 214, Milwaukee, WI 53233.

Quarterly publication in tabloid newspaper format. Helpful source of information for singles and group leaders, sent free for a donation and to all members of the association, who pay annual dues. A leadership-level membership also includes other resources and benefits, including the *Single i* newsletter mentioned above.

IX. SELECTED PROGRAM RESOURCES

The following are some of the programs that have been reviewed in the process of developing the programs at Good News Community. Some readers may wish to contact these sources for alternative resources to help develop their own programs for local needs.

The Beginning Experience. Central Office, 3100 West 41st Street, Sioux Falls, SD 57105-4294.

A weekend format in use around the country by both Catholic and Protestant organizations. Information on how leaders can become certified available from Fr. Guy Gau, director.

Coping With Divorce. Good News Community, 4319 Byron Center Avenue S.W., Grand Rapids, MI 49509.

An 8½-x-11 manual for the program described in chapter 6 of this book, containing additional practical helps and photocopy masters of discussion sheets, as well as other related materials.

Beginning Again. Merit Books, Merit Media International, P.O. Box 3319, Laguna Hills, CA 92654.

Developed by Terry Hershey, author of the book *Beginning Again.* Includes a program manual, cassettes, and related materials.

Divorce Recovery Workshop. Positive Christian Singles, Crystal Cathedral, Chapman at Lewis, Garden Grove, CA 92640.

Materials that served as the forerunner of the Beginning Again program listed above. Terry Hershey's cassettes for this program possibly still available.

A Fresh Start. Church of the Saviour, 751 North Wayne Avenue, Wayne, PA 19087.

A weekend program designed by Bob Burns, singles pastor, as only one part of a variety of programs for singles at the church. Burns and volunteer staff available to conduct workshops and provide materials for other churches for a modest fee. However, they wish to limit these training experiences to churches committed to a continuous and well-rounded ministry to single and divorced people rather than an occasional or one-shot effort.

Rebuilding. Family Learning Relations Center, 450 Ord Drive, Boulder, CO 80303.

Bruce Fisher, director. A source of materials for seminar and a book published under the same name. Can provide the Fisher Divorce Adjustment Scale and related literature.